NLP - Skills for

A practical handbook for increasing learning potential

Peter Freeth

Published by

Communications In Action

NLP - Skills for Learning

ISBN 0-954-57480-X

Communications In Action 2003

Published by:

Communications In Action
49 Fishponds Road
Kenilworth
Warwickshire
CV8 1EY
United Kingdom

First Edition - July 2003, reprinted November 2004

www.ciauk.com   0870 1620802
peter@ciauk.com   +44 870 1620802

Printed and bound by Antony Rowe Ltd, Eastbourne

Ingredients

This handbook contains at least the recommended daily allowance of intellectual stimulation, good humour and useful reference material for the modern learning professional. Used regularly, this handbook will help you enjoy developing your skills for learning.

What's it all about?

NLP is nothing more than the study of excellence. Many years ago, some people created a formal structure for extracting the intuitive talent that is deeply embedded within the minds of outstanding people. That talent can be refined and improved, and also taught to other people.

Think of someone who does something that you admire, and they make it look so easy. Ask them how they learned to do it and there's a good chance that they will say, "I don't know how, I just do it". Whilst you can learn a lot from people like this, it usually takes a long time because they can't explain how they are thinking. They think that everyone can do what they do.

NLP gives us a structure and a language for sharing intuitive knowledge. We can use it to model the expertise of anyone who excels at anything.

So, if you know someone who is an outstanding trainer, presenter, speaker, learner, teacher or just a fabulous person, you can use the NLP toolkit to model and copy their expertise.

The modelling process itself isn't the subject of this handbook, as there are many other excellent books that will tell you about it. Many, many excellent communicators have already been modelled and their expertise is available to you through this handbook, which doesn't require you to learn about NLP unless you want to and doesn't require you to go on a training course and then figure it all out for yourself.

NLP can help you to unlock the potential in what you already do. As a successful, competent trainer you can become an outstanding, inspirational trainer. You don't have to learn anything new to do that - you just refine and align the talents that are already within you.

This handbook is for anyone who wants access to the results that NLP will help them achieve, without having to spend a lot of time learning about NLP.

Up until now, there are really two ways that you, as a teacher, coach, trainer, facilitator or learning enabler could acquire NLP skills. You could read one of the handful of books on the subject, which are built for length rather than comfort and assume you want to know everything there is to know about NLP. Alternatively, you could go to a NLP Practitioner course and learn all about the fundamental principles of NLP. You would then have to apply these principles to the area of training yourself.

The principles that underpin NLP tools such as phobia cures are actually very useful in helping people learn, you just aren't explicitly told how in any NLP training that I've ever seen, and I've seen more than many people.

NLP in its purest form is all about personal excellence and is characterised by a curiosity about people and how they move through the world. NLP training will definitely help you become a more capable, effective person. It will help you to set goals, realise your dreams and communicate effectively with other people. If you think this is far-fetched, I suggest you don't knock it until you've tried it. If you've tried it and hated it I will assume you're not reading this book and I'm talking to myself. On the whole, the people I've seen go through Practitioner training describe it as a transformational experience. Just don't assume that everyone wants to be transformed.

After reading this - and perhaps after coming to the one day masterclass that goes with it - you may decide that NLP is something you would like to learn more about. You may even decide to become a licensed NLP Practitioner. If this is the case then spend some time choosing a trainer who you are personally comfortable with, as the Practitioner course is a very personal experience. It is not a load of stuff to learn, it is an experience to work through and reflect upon. You will not be taught anything, but you will be given many opportunities to notice what is happening and learn from your own experience. You will, of course, learn about the tools and techniques of NLP, but these are only the results of NLP - they are not NLP in themselves.

NLP is full of jargon, and some of it is a bit unnecessary. There's even a special word for "talking to myself". This is not a book of NLP jargon. This is a book of plain language that I hope you will pick up and understand immediately. NLP was not created in a cave in Tibet, it was created by modelling real people like you. Therefore, you already know how to do everything that NLP can teach you. What you may not achieve right now is consistency, and this is the main area where people benefit from NLP training. There are many things that you do better than anyone else on the planet, and there are many things that someone else does better than you. By "better" I mean more easily and with more consistent results.

If you already have NLP experience then this handbook will give you some ready made applications for many of the things you will have learned about.

If you have no idea what NLP is then you can just take what's in this book at face value, use it and get better results straight away. It really is that simple.

One more thing - this book is written in much the same way that I run training courses. Some information flows forwards, some flows backwards and some flows sideways. This way of layering information makes for very powerful, long term learning. You will find ideas or concepts hinted at and then explained in full later on. You may also find them explained in full first and then hinted at later. You may even find that some concepts assemble themselves out of pieces that turn up in different chapters. I ask you to take this book as a whole, as many of the chapters link together in different ways to form a complete learning experience. This book isn't just about NLP; it *is* NLP - in action. You'll find anchoring, hypnotic language and stories embedded in the words that are deigned to create as lifelike a learning experience as you can get from a book.

Every book I've ever seen about NLP is just that - it describes NLP without letting you experience it. As you read this book, pay attention to any stray daydreams or ideas you get. Pay attention to the thoughts you have about the way you will apply what you are learning here. After you have read the whole book, you may find new connections being made. The book is a bit like a jigsaw puzzle, you need to see the whole thing in order to work out what the picture is. This isn't done to be clever - it's crafted to fully exploit your amazing, individual learning potential.

As you will already know, people learn in different ways. There are many different ways of putting learning styles into categories - maybe 4, 6, 8 or even 16 categories depending on which scheme you favour. Well, here's the twist. In fact, there are around 6 billion different learning styles. Unfortunately, the amazing diversity of the human capacity for learning is a bit too complicated for the people who sell profiling tests, so they generalise that diversity into a handful of categories and force people into them based on a few symptoms.

Once "they" know what your learning style is, you're only allowed to learn that way. Thoughtful training providers will structure their delivery for different learning styles. Does this mean that you can only ever learn in one way? No! You can, and do, learn any way you like. Don't let anyone stop you.

A book that incorporates learning styles could have some practical exercises for you, some theory, it could even have some blank pages for you to write your own thoughts on as you reflect on what you have read. This book, on the other hand, uses everything that we know today about powerful learning to help you take in information through this relatively limited medium. I've even tried out a few ideas, which, to the best of my knowledge, have never been tried before, anywhere. By using NLP as it's explained, you get at least twice the opportunity to learn, whatever your preference.

So, why Skills for Learning and not Skills for Training or Skills for Trainers? The answer to that lies in the job that we do. I get very frustrated at the prevalence of training centres, resources for trainers and people who think that presenting is the same as training or teaching. When I use a training centre, the staff there focus on me and giving me what I need – boxes of pens, flipcharts, trainer packs, discounts and so on.

This frustrates me because I want them to focus on giving my learners what they want. I'm providing a service to the people who are on the course and that's who I want the centre managers to focus on too. I want a great learning environment, good food and refreshments, good accommodation and a room with a flexible layout. Recently I had to physically cut a power cable for an OHP out of a floor box in the centre of the room so that we didn't trip over it. Obviously all trainers use OHPs in the centre of the room with delegates neatly arranged in quiet, studious rows.

Simply, the training industry revolves around making life easy for the trainer. I think we trainers shouldn't mind working a little harder to make life easier for our learners!

I met someone recently who wanted all the courses run by a local college to have standardised presentation slides so that a stand-in trainer could run the course if the usual trainer was ill. This is a great idea to ensure delegates are not disappointed by unavoidable last minute mishaps, however the slides are not the course – the course is the learning experience, not the material. Don't confuse a record of the trainer's words with the learning experience itself.

Some people confuse the job of a trainer with that of a presenter, even though they are not the same. A presenter's job is to transmit information – think of a TV or conference presenter, for example. A trainer's job is to make sure that information gets into the delegates' brains, stays there and transforms into behaviour.

So the most important person is the learner. They are doing all the hard work. All the trainer, teacher or coach does is facilitate that – make it easy for the learner to learn. That's what this book is about.

The most important thing you can do after reading this book is....anything! Don't read another book, don't sit and ponder, go and do something. Start playing with what you've learned. Don't try, or plan or plot - just play. Have fun, enjoy yourself, and your learners will enjoy themselves too.

I've summarised some of the key points in this handbook so that you can pick them out more easily.

 The exclamation mark is there to draw your attention to really important points that may seem simple or obvious, yet by paying special attention to them you will learn more about yourself and other people and your skills will improve dramatically. It's easy to overlook the obvious things in life, yet sometimes they hold hidden treasures.

So, if you see that symbol, just take a moment to think about the point as there may be relevance or importance in it that's easy to take for granted or overlook.

They say that the simple things in life are the best, and in the case of these important points, it's true. Or is it that the best things in life are free?

Often, books give you a lot of information which is factually correct and informative, but which may not be related to your specific interests or needs.

 A "so what?" is a summary of a key point, specific to the application of the information in a learning context. If you've ever read something which seems very important but totally irrelevant you may have wanted to ask the author this question. I hope to put some of the theory of NLP into practical terms that you can use every day to get better results.

What equipment do you have for gathering information about the world?

Obviously, I can't hear you, so I'll pretend you said "Your five senses!!"

And I'll say "well done!"….sort of. In that there are more than five. Here are some of the senses that you have - there may be more as we find out more about neurology and the way that your brain handles sensory information that is outside of our conscious perception. Here are just a few of them.….

Now, this might appear to be obvious, and therefore trivial, but it is in fact the most important thing you will learn today.

Why? Because we must now accept that all of the rich memories, ideas, thoughts, pictures, sounds, poems, songs and desires that are in your head got there by coming in through your senses. They didn't appear mystically and they didn't arrive through intuition.

You might think that this is obvious, but it has an important meaning for our communication. The colour green, the sound of a car horn and the smell of lemon juice are easy to think of in terms of sensory inputs. What about honesty, professionalism and danger? What do these mean in sensory terms? What exactly does honesty sound like?

 Almost everything that is in your head got there through your senses. Therefore, your senses are what you use to represent memories to yourself.

You see, hear, feel, taste and smell memories using the same processing systems that allow you to gather real time information from the outside world.

Almost everything? Yes, except for certain instinctive knowledge that you were born with, such as how to breathe, beat your heart or swallow milk. If you remember that far back then you'll know that it took you a while to learn how to regulate your body temperature and even longer to learn how to move, walk and speak.

Our senses are our only tool for interacting with the world, yet as we grow older we ignore sensory information more and more and replace it with 'experience' or what we 'know'. It will help you a great deal to gather more information if you try and forget what you think you already know. Intuition is one way that you notice subtle sensory information that gets missed in the fog of all the stuff you 'know' about.

Intuition is not mystical. It is the magic of your brain working far faster and more powerfully than you could ever think possible. It is the product of the amazing ability of your brain to gather and process both real time and stored information and produce something new and remarkable in the blink of an eye.

Of course, you may be unconsciously aware of sensory information that is outside of our normal awareness, so this may also play a part in what we call "intuition". For example, we have a sense of direction which, like in migrating birds, detects the Earth's magnetic field.

So, if you thought intuition was great, the natural function of your brain is even more amazing! But this isn't a book on neurology. It's a book on the practical applications of this knowledge, so let's get back to those senses.

Over the years, you have taken in vast amounts of sensory data and attached linguistic labels to it. We don't fully understand this process, so as a consequence we can't get computers to copy it. We can teach a computer to understand that an object is both a table and wood, but if we smash the table up the computer struggles to understand that whilst it's still wood, it's not a table anymore.

In fact, we still can't even get computers to recognise faces reliably. Whereas you can recognise someone you haven't seen in years, a computer can't even recognise the same person with a hat on. It's not through a lack of computer power or programming skill – it's because we don't understand how the human mind does it.

I recently read a review of biometric security devices for computers which included retina scanners and fingerprint readers. The fingerprint reader could be fooled with a jelly baby. So, no matter how amazing you find modern technology, there is still nothing to touch the computer between your ears.

You may have heard that you have a left brain and a right brain, or that you have a conscious and an unconscious brain, or that you have different thinking modes, or that you have an inner eye. All of this may or may not be true, depending on how you look at it. The coloured tint in your spectacles gives you a certain view of the world which may or may not be different to everyone else's.

You may be thinking, "I see the world clearly and objectively, so the fault must lie with other people". Well, the bad news is that there is no objectivity.

Have you ever lost your car keys, only to find them right in front of you? Have you ever pushed a door that was clearly marked "PULL"?

Can you see the dots changing from white to grey to black as you look around the picture?

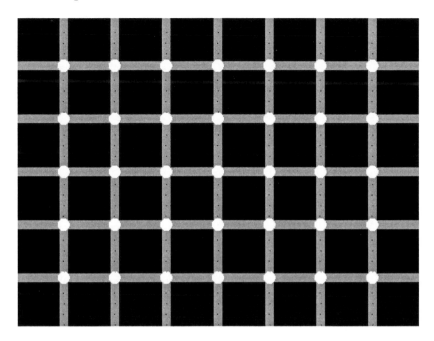

Do the horizontal lines look curved or straight?

Have you ever heard someone say something totally different to what they actually said? Have you ever daydreamed? Have you ever dreamed at night?

Well, if you answered "Yes!" to any of those, where did that voice come from? Was it the one in your head? Don't worry, we've all got one. Some of us have many, and they can come in very handy.

Here's the first useful tip for you. It may not be directly related to training but I can guarantee it is a very useful thing to know about. In fact, if you ever feel nervous or if you ever worry, or if you ever tell yourself you should have known better, then this will be a very, very useful thing to know. Are you ready?

Did you know that you have total conscious control over that voice in your head?

Did you know that if it nags you or criticises you, you can change its tone of voice to be anything you want. If it sounded really soothing and supportive, would you be more inclined to listen to its advice?

If it sounded really excited and enthusiastic, how do you think you would feel? Try it out now.....In a really critical, harsh voice, say, "That was rubbish, you should have known better". Next, use a really kind and supportive voice to say "Hey! That didn't work so well, what can you do differently next time?" Pay attention to the difference in how you feel about those two voices.

 You can change the qualities of the voice inside your head. You can make it sound supportive, you can make it sound like a newsreader, you can make it sound like a cartoon character. Any of these will change your emotional state and allow you to benefit from the feedback from your internal commentator. In fact, you can change the qualities of any of your sensory systems to change the emotional content of memories.

Just so you're familiar with the NLP jargon, the voice inside your head is called your 'Internal Dialogue'. Other people have taken the idea and renamed it "self talk" and a dozen other things. They all mean the same thing – talking to yourself using the voice that only you can hear inside your head. Of course, some people talk to themselves out loud, but it's the same thing.

If you find that you criticise yourself when you get things wrong and that this makes you feel bad, just try this really simple exercise.

Next time you make a mistake and the voice says "that was stupid" or "that was a bad idea" say, in a genuinely curious way, "Thankyou! Now, how does that information help me?" You can try any variation on this, such as "Thankyou! What do you suggest I do differently next time?" You will find that the results are quite different to when you just nag yourself. You can make up any form of words that are right for you as long as you follow the basic structure of "acknowledge value" then "redirect to a positive course of action". You probably already apply this structure when other people offer you criticism - don't you? It just helps bypass the emotion of criticism and get to the real value - the feedback.

You may say "but this doesn't apply to me" in which case you should pay twice as much attention. When you're in a learning environment, some people will beat themselves up for making "mistakes". You'll know when they do this from listening to what they say, for example "I told myself I should have known better" or "I said to myself that this was wrong". When you hear this, you can constructively intervene by helping them change their internal dialogue.

So, what we know now is that everything you know is represented to you using one or more of your senses. For example, you 'know' the colour of your front door by seeing a picture of it. We also know that your senses may not be giving you the full picture, the whole story or a real handle on the situation. This is a very useful thing for you to know as a professional communicator (and who isn't?)

OK, so I skipped about and covered quite a few subjects there, so to summarise:

The only way that you can gather information about the world is through your senses. As you get older and have more experiences, you filter your senses more and more and over time what you think you see, hear and feel about the world gets further away from reality. Often, this is a good thing and helps you to deal with the huge amount of sensory information that comes into your brain every moment of every day and night. Your biggest step forward as a professional communicator and learning enabler will be when you realise this and simply start paying more attention to what is outside than what is inside.

You could be amazed at the amount of information that is all around you if you take the trouble to pay attention. Instead of thinking that you know what other people are thinking or what their motives are - ask them! Instead of guessing, pay attention! Instead of knowing, forget and enjoy the experience of sampling the world through fresh eyes and ears.

On the radio today I heard an interviewee say, "There are no absolutes" and it made me smile. What, none at all? Not one? Not even one about there being no absolutes?

By listening to what people say, you will learn a great deal about the way that their internal world is organised. NLP training can teach you all the details of the Milton Model, the Meta Model, conversational postulates and unspecified nouns but the truth is that NLP came out of a set of beliefs from people who were gifted or talented communicators. They didn't stop what they were doing and say to themselves "ooh...I should use a tag question next, shouldn't I?" You don't have to learn the way that this knowledge has been categorised and indexed, you only need to share their enthusiasm for learning more about other people.

When you went to school and learned about nouns and verbs, you didn't start speaking differently - you simply acquired a new labelling system for what you already knew about. That labelling system only serves the purpose of letting two or more people share information using a common language.

All of the linguistic stuff in NLP is very powerful but you should regard it only as a framework to refine the way you already use language. You'll be amazed at the way you already influence people. Recently, I was watching a training session where the teacher (it was in a school) was running an exercise in which groups of students had to build a model roller coaster using card stuck to a hardboard panel. As she gave out the first panel she said to the first group "Here's your board" upon which one of the students collapsed, comatose, onto his folded arms on the table. The teacher shouted "Oi! Wake up, sit up straight, pay attention" and so on. Well, what did she expect? If she insists on going round hypnotising people then she has to accept the results she gets. Why?

Your brain uses context to derive the most likely meaning from similar sounding words. Whilst you extract the most contextually likely meaning at the conscious level, at the unconscious level you run through all possible meanings. If one of them is expressed as an instruction, there's a good chance you will act upon it.

Having sat in a classroom all day, if someone said to you "You're bored" then what meaning would you take from it?

In this example, the teacher needs to call her piece of hardboard a sheet, a base, a panel - just anything other than "board"!

Just think about the impact of this for a moment. Every day, all over the world, there are groups of important people shaping our future by meeting in "Board Rooms" Mind you, having sat through some bored meetings I think the name is very appropriate!

Taking it all in

The world we live in is a busy, busy place. In fact, the world has always been busy and there's more information available than we can consciously attend to. I don't mean information like news, TV etc. I mean sensory stimuli - things that you can see, hear, feel, taste and smell. Right now, you can see these words, you might also be reading to yourself using the voice in your head. You might also be aware of any background noise. Are you aware of the temperature of the air? How about the weight of your hands? How about that itch? Are you hungry? Thirsty? Tired?

You could think of your unconscious brain as your car's engine management computer and your conscious brain as your car's instrument panel. Normally, you don't need to know what's going on under the bonnet. If there's a problem, a warning light comes on. You don't need to know the status of every muscle in your body except for if there's a problem in which case you get a pain. Another useful analogy is that your unconscious brain is a dark room and your conscious attention is a torch.

The unconscious brain is, of course, the same brain as your conscious brain. The conscious bit is everything that you are aware of, and that will change from one second to another. You might be so engrossed in this book that you are unaware of any background noise until I call your attention to it. At least, I hope you're engrossed!

At any moment, you can attend to only a handful of thoughts. In NLP, these thoughts are called 'chunks' and refer to things like short term memory and activities. Try juggling and remembering a telephone number at the same time, and you'll start to understand the limitations of your conscious attention. You already knew about breaking a task down into smaller chunks, and now you know how it works too.

In a driving example, this would be like practising gear changes until you could change gear without thinking about it - then move onto the next element. I believe that a really good way to learn something like driving would be to run through specific behavioural sequences until they become one "chunk" of information. For example, changing gear and working the clutch pedal at the same time is very difficult to start off with, although the motor movement in your arm and leg is not very complex. If that movement was already "natural" when you first got into a car, putting together the individual movements and patterns would be a lot easier than trying to learn it all at the same time, under pressure. Driving simulators are a huge step forward as they remove the pressure and allow the learner to practice the basics.

 People will often find it very difficult to learn a new skill, simply because the volume of sensory information being presented overwhelms their conscious processing power. Break the task down and build the learning experience in layers. You could break it down by sensory system, i.e. start by watching, then hearing, then feeling. You could also break it down by time, so either start slowly and speed up, or break apart the components of the activity that normally take place at the same time.

Your ability to focus your attention is both a gift and a drawback, depending on the activity you're trying to master. If you are training people to remember something complex, they will simply be unable to process everything that is happening. For an experienced driver, the whole business of driving is mostly under unconscious control so an experienced driver can drive and hold a conversation at the same time. A learner driver needs to attend consciously to every individual component of operating a car, and there is simply too much going on. If the learner is also trying to attend to feelings of stress, hunger or thirst, the conscious brain will simply be overloaded and they will not learn anything at all. For an experienced driver, "change gear" is one chunk. For a learner, it is about six.

You may have heard that words only make up part of communication. According to the social psychologists Mehrabian and Argyle, words only make up 7% of communication. Whether you agree with the figure or not, we can at least agree that words are not the only form of communication and that there are times when words are misleading.

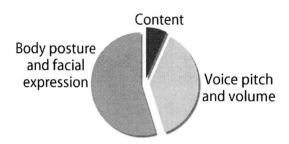

Content

Body posture and facial expression

Voice pitch and volume

Do you know when someone is lying? How? Well, if you don't already know then I'll tell you. Your brain is analysing all forms of communication while consciously you are attending to the words. Your brain compares the content - the words - to facial expression, body posture, voice pitch, speech rate, volume, stability etc. and finds that the two don't match up. Your brain alerts you to this through a 'gut feeling' or an instinctive reaction - you can call it intuition if you want to. You might say something like "Something he said didn't ring true" or "I don't like the look of him" or even "it was written all over his face".

When we take in information, we filter it to allow our conscious attention to focus on what seems relevant. The process of filtering works in three different ways, so that we delete, distort and generalise incoming information.

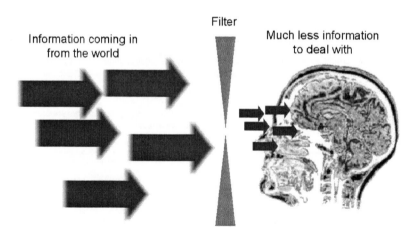

Filter

Information coming in from the world

Much less information to deal with

So, when communicating with a group of people, it's important to remember that they are all gathering information differently to each other and to you. They will only be attending to a small part of the information you give them. The more ways that you can deliver the same information, the more chance there is that they will find something of value to them, process it and remember it.

If lunchtime is approaching, people are not listening to you regardless of the value of the information you are trying to impart. You may use this knowledge to communicate directly with their unconscious minds, but you're probably better off taking an early lunch. Longer break times do not equate to less learning. Some people need time to reflect on what they are learning, otherwise they are not able to form long term connections with the new material. Longer breaks allow these people more time to reflect and absorb what they are learning. Whatever you do, people will find a meaning in it.

Years and years ago, I gave my first big, formal presentation at a conference. I stood on a stage, behind a lectern and in the glare of a spotlight. There was a big screen behind me with someone working the back projector when I pressed a button. I wanted it to go really well, so I wrote myself a script. The only problem was that halfway through the presentation I lost my place and read the same paragraph twice. Filled with dread, I finished my presentation just before a break.

Over coffee, a colleague of mine told me that the presentation had gone well to which I replied "Oh no! It was terrible, I read the same paragraph twice and it was awful". My colleague said, "Oh, I thought you did that because it was a really important bit". In fact, one person in the audience who was getting a little sleepy after lunch even thought I was talking just to him to wake him up!

It just goes to show that even with the best planning in the world, people will infer any meaning they choose regardless of what you do. The frame of reference that you create has a far bigger impact on this meaning than anything else you do. Because I was on stage, I took on the role of an expert who must plan methodically and have a reason for everything. People found meanings that fitted their frame of reference.

Of course, some people thought "he just repeated that, he must be nervous" but the important thing is that nobody cared except for me.

People have an interesting way of inferring meaning from everything you do, and it's usually much kinder than the meaning you attach.

 Setting the frame of reference at the start is the single most important step you can take in creating powerful learning, as the audience will search for meanings that are relevant within that frame. After this point, anything that you do, within reason, will reinforce the learning.

This goes much further than "tell them what you're going to tell them". If you start by setting the agenda, people in the audience will immediately run through it ahead of you, decide what they are going to pay attention to and then switch off. It's important that you make the agenda loose enough that the audience cannot decide by themselves what is important. In fact, an agenda written from a pure learning point of view might be:

1. Introductions
2. Learn some great stuff
3. Break
4. Learn more great stuff
5. Lunch
6. Learn amazing stuff
7. Break
8. Amaze yourselves with all the stuff you've learned
9. Close

That might be taking the idea a bit far, but remember that an agenda is just a summary of what the presentation contains. As people gather information, they compress it down, make it less complicated and forget most of it. By starting with an explicit agenda, you have already summarised your entire course onto one slide and many people will stop learning at that point.

If you absolutely must use an agenda, then at least make it sound interesting. Tell people what they will be able to do, rather than what you will talk about.

Personally, I can't think of a situation where you really need an agenda. You might think that you at least need to tell people break times. If you do, they'll be clock watching and thinking about the telephone calls they need to make.

You'll find that some people are desperate to be told what they're going to learn about, and you now know many ways to handle this effectively.

Instead, you can tell people that there will be short, regular breaks with more than enough time to attend to matters outside of the presentation room. Take breaks, not because the agenda says so but because you and the audience need them. Some training environments are so good you don't need to take a break all day long. Others are so bad that you need a break every half hour. Leave yourself the flexibility you need to keep your audience in a great learning state.

If you don't agree break times up front, people will not come back on time, will they? Well, some people will be late back whatever you do. I suggest you deal with this when you set the frame at the start of the session. Try something like "We're going to take regular short breaks throughout the day and each time we take a break I will tell you the time that I will restart. If you're not back in the room at that time I will assume that, at that moment, you have something important that you need to do and that's OK with me. I would rather you take care of important matters when you need to so that when we are in this room together, we can all concentrate fully on what we are learning here."

So, bear in mind that people have a limited focus of attention. I read somewhere that young children can concentrate for about five minutes, and that this attention span gets longer as we get older. Personally, I don't think this ever changes. Instead, adults just devise ingenious strategies for appearing to pay attention when in fact they're thinking about something else.

So, you can get upset when people don't pay attention, or you can accept it as entirely normal and work with it, using it to your advantage to get better results with your learners.

State

Now that we've covered some background, we can move into some even more useful, practical stuff. Whenever you set out to do anything - read a book, deliver a presentation, go to a meeting, relax or go to sleep, you probably have a routine for getting yourself into the right frame of mind. Perhaps you start to do something important and then postpone it because there are other things on your mind that you need to attend to first.

Being in the right state is the first and most important step in achieving anything. This doesn't mean that you should be happy all the time, as those emotions we often label as "negative" can be just as useful for achieving certain outcomes. The point is that you choose the emotional state which will get you the best results, not that you choose the best emotional state.

Really effective people are very good at choosing states, moving into them quickly and exploiting their power. Every state, from anger through to apathy, has a purpose and the potential to help you achieve your chosen outcome. Of course, that implies that you have a chosen outcome, which we'll come onto later. Suffice to say that really effective people naturally decide what it is they want and choose their outcomes very well. They go on to achieve those outcomes more often than the average man in the street, too.

There are essentially two ways to quickly change your emotional and mental state - changing your focus of attention and changing your physiology. Later on, there are some quick exercises that you can use to control focus of attention for yourself and your learners. You can even set a trigger for a state, giving you fast and easy access to it in future.

For now, we'll stick to physiology as it's really simple, really powerful and really easy to ignore. If you are alert and have plenty of water and oxygen, you will feel energetic and perform well. If you are lacking in any basic physiological needs such as sleep and light, you will perform below your best.

Hmmm…..Well, there's nothing new there. In fact, this isn't even NLP, but it's worth saying anyway. In fact, there is some NLP in here - once you get into rapport with your audience, you will affect each other's states. If you get tired after lunch, they will. If they get bored, you will. It's worth practicing getting out of rapport with people and finding a way to alert yourself to the onset of tiredness, because we usually don't notice until it's too late.

Getting the right physiology for learning is the first thing you can do to improve the state of your learners. In a warm, cramped room with no natural light, you'll be lucky to keep your learners awake, let alone in a learning state.

In a room with lots of fresh air, light and water, even an average presenter can keep the audience in an attentive state. There is absolutely no good reason for making life hard for yourself, so get the environment right first before you think about anything else.

Aside from this, there isn't a right learning environment, and there isn't a right colour for learning. Rather than trying to second guess the needs and preferences of your audience, go for a venue that you feel comfortable in, so that you're relaxed and your confident state can rub off on your audience.

You can design exercises that require people to physically move in order to complete them. I don't mean building steam engines out of tin cans or struggling with radioactive waste, I mean standing up and moving around, going to other rooms and talking. Getting people to change their physical posture periodically is a great way for you to manage their learning state.

Outcomes

People who are very good at getting what they want are very good at understanding a simple secret to success. Here it is - you are more likely to get what you want if you know what you want. These people are very good at setting goals for themselves in a special way which programs the brain to notice opportunities automatically.

Knowing what you want makes it far easier to achieve. Successful people know this intuitively and use a simple formula to turn their goals into reality. You can copy this formula to get the results you want.

Later on, there's a formula you can use for setting goals that makes them easier to achieve. It's quite obvious really, the goal has to be something you want rather than something you don't want, you need to know exactly what it will look, sound, feel, taste and smell like, and achieving the goal needs to be good for you with no unwanted side effects.

You can use this simple formula in a number of ways to help people learn effectively. Sometimes, we learn by planning what we're going to learn and sometimes we learn spontaneously. Recent research by Tina Cook (a friend of mine!) suggests that both are necessary for effective learning.

Often, the purpose of learning is inferred by the course title. Since the course title usually reflects the needs of the learner, it can sometimes create confusion because it describes the problem rather than the solution. I recommend you create course titles that reflect what learners will be able to do, rather than the problem you are helping them solve. In reality, a good title or headline would have both in it.

Some time ago, I did some work with a group of trainers who specialised in stress management. Their problem was that delegates would often be disruptive and uncooperative and they found it difficult to hold the course together. The first thing that jumped out was the title of the course - "Stress Management". It's a very common title for that type of course, but it describes the problem. When you add in the fact that many people on the course had been "sent" by their managers, the meaning became "You're stressed and you're not managing it". No wonder some people were reluctant to take part, as the problem was not necessarily their ability to manage their state but perhaps more to do with the workload imposed by the boss. The manager was effectively saying "I don't like you getting upset when I pile more work on you". Did the staff need a stress management course, or does the manager need a time management course?

Instead of Stress Management, how about State Management? A bit vague. Instead of just letting people manage stress, how about having them grab it by the horns? Stress Control? Stress Engineering? How about having a Stress Rodeo? Yee-Haa! It certainly creates a different impression, and that's what is important.

A key factor in what we might call accelerated learning is individuality. If you have training content where uniformity is important such as Health and Safety or regulatory training, it's important that you use what you know about outcomes to set the frame of reference and tell people what they are going to do with their new knowledge.

If your training topic is more open, you can have the audience create individual learning outcomes which will define individual frames of reference. They are then far more likely to learn something which is useful and relevant to them and which transfers easily back to the workplace.

If you are doing something with personal development, it can be useful to run through the well formed outcomes exercise at the start of the course, using their own learning objectives as an exercise topic. This will force them to create learning objectives if they didn't already have them, and they will achieve those objectives as the course progresses.

If you want to use this same tool in a more indirect way, you can use a feedback form that the delegates fill in at the start of the course.

Here's an example that I use. I tell the course delegates that since I'm sure they want to rush away at the end of the course we'll fill in the feedback form at the start to save time later.

Communications In Action

What do you want to get out of this workshop?

What can you see yourself doing differently as a result of this workshop?

What one thing will you tell your friends that you enjoyed most about the workshop?

What do you want to learn from this workshop?

How will you know when you've learned it?

What will having learned that do for you?

When will be your first opportunity to practice what you've learned?

What difference will other people notice in you at this next opportunity?

Actually, here's an important point about real feedback forms – I often get delegates to fill them in during lunchtime or afternoon break because they have really seen all they need to – the course isn't going to get any better from that point on! And then they're in a much better state to give high quality feedback rather than rushing through the form because they want to get away.

The feedback form I use at the start of a course is essentially one big future pace (a kind of vivid daydream about the future) that's loaded with presuppositions about the value of the course and the way that delegates will transfer and apply what they've learned. It allows learners to build on their own experience and thereby get the most complete, useful learning experience possible.

A presupposition is a very special linguistic tool in NLP that works on the basis that we process language by holding certain concepts as true in order to make sense of the words. The neat thing about a presupposition is that by the time the listener hears it, it's already too late. A presupposition is not a NLP invention – it's a grammatical concept. As with most things, NLP simply adds some purpose to the use of presuppositions so that instead of influencing people randomly, you do so in a directed, consistent and helpful way.

Later on, you'll read about something called "well formed outcomes", which is essentially a way to program your brain to notice opportunities for you to achieve your goals. You can use the outcomes exercise as it is, as it's a really useful thing for a delegate to take away from any training course. Alternatively, you can build the concept and language of the exercise into anything you do.

For example, you can ask delegates how they see themselves using what they've learned, or you can ask them what they see as they use what they've learned. Whilst these sound the same, they in fact generate completely different internal mental processes.

For example, asking them what other people will notice forces them to imagine something changing, which in turn creates the possibility for change. They may or may not change, what's important is that they are more open minded.

What's really important is that you prepare your delegates for an outstanding learning experience, and the simplest way to do this is to tell them to expect just that!

Rapport

You already know what rapport is. It's that thing you have with people you like, when you're on the same wavelength, see eye to eye and feel a real connection with them.

You can think of rapport as being a conduit for effective communication. Without it, it's very difficult to engage the processes of agreement and compliance. In other words, people are more likely to do what you want if they like you.

This is, of course, as plain as the nose on your face. You might have a very fancy nose, but however fancy or plain your nose is, that's how obvious the need for rapport is.

Having said that, and assuming that you're a naturally likeable and gregarious person, there are still many things that people do to stifle natural rapport.

The most common in the context of training and presenting seems to be the placing of barriers between the audience and the speaker. A lectern blocks the audience's view of the speaker and restricts the flow of non-verbal information - a key component in establishing rapport. Without rapport, the audience loses interest, the speaker gets nervous and the relationship descends in a spiral of infectious states.

The first and most important thing is to be in rapport with yourself. Self doubt and confusion lead to incongruence that the audience will pick up on instantly. They may not recognise it consciously but they will still find it hard to accept what you say. When you're in an incongruent state, you're more likely to generate confusion and doubt in the audience. You may choose to do this, in which case incongruence is a very useful tool.

In general, in most situations, it is more useful to have rapport than not. You can practice all the body language stuff, matching and mirroring body posture and echoing voice tone, but how do you do that with a group of people?

The simplest answer is don't bother. If you are congruent and friendly, you will find that the audience gradually gets into rapport with you. You'll know the experience of getting the audience "on your side" and you may also notice the moment when that happens. What you can start to notice is what exactly you do that makes that change happen. When the audience's state shifts, what did you do that made it shift?

Rapport is a very good indicator of group compliance and you will find that when you raise subjects which are contentious or engage opinion, the audience splits into smaller groups. Pay attention to who shifts first and who follows them and you will learn everything you need to know about the hierarchical power structure of the group.

Most of the time, we get into and out of rapport with people unconsciously, so our beliefs and thoughts are revealed non-verbally, regardless of our efforts to hide our true feelings.

If there's one simple thing you can learn about rapport, it's that you can choose the people you want to get into rapport with. If you feel that a salesman is being a bit too persuasive, or that someone secretly disagrees with you, even though they say differently, then it's worth having a quick check of your state to see what's going on.

You have probably heard of "body language" as devised by Allan Pease in the 1970s. Personally, I think that this came from an era where psychologists thought that people's behaviour could be neatly packaged and explained with clear cause and effect. For example, if you put your hands behind your head, you're being arrogant. I think that the idea of body language is helpful in that it gets people to think of their physical state as a means of communication, but it's not helpful to think of specific gestures as having specific meanings.

Of course, Pease neatly got round this with the idea of 'clusters', so to have your hands behind your head is arrogant, unless you blink and twitch your toe, in which case it could mean anything. I think Pease's basic premise here is fine, but he stretches it too far in search of a simplified theory that he can apply to all humans. Once again, we fall into the trap of believing generalisations to be true.

Just a quick aside – generalisations become true because of the way our brain filters information. Therefore when you use words like everyone, people, always, all or everything, your listeners will automatically apply what you're saying to them. Everyone does this so it's nothing to worry about, it's just part of the way our brains create a model of the world that's simple enough for us to interact with. Because everyone does this, we are all able to learn from it by sharing our generalisations. It's a useful thing to do on a training course when you're exploring complex yet vague issues such as "respect" or "professionalism" or even "sales and marketing". Everyone has their own definition of these terms and it's important to start with a common frame of reference. Now, back to the main feature.

I believe that Pease's basic premise is that some gestures have some socially learned basis, such as the 'thumbs up', whilst others are unique to the individual. Therefore, a lazy communicator could learn to recognise generic gestures in order to understand non-verbal communication. Of course, it's more accurate to say that everyone understands non-verbal communication because it's not separate from verbal communication - it's all part of the same information flow.

Therefore, we all understand non-verbal communication, but we are consciously aware of its meaning to different levels. At one end of the spectrum, some people need a slap in the face to pick up on unspoken information, whilst people at the other end of the spectrum are now said to have a high EQ, or Emotional Intelligence quotient. Whilst you may or may not believe in EI, there's no doubt it has helped revive interest in good old fashioned people skills.

You've probably heard about sales training courses where people are taught to "match" or "mirror" the way that their customers stand or sit in order to get into rapport. There are certainly some interesting things you can learn from doing this, and there are a few rapport exercises at the end of this handbook that you can play with, but personally I don't recommend you actually advise training delegates to do this in real life.

Personally, I think it's a bit contrived to adjust your "body language" to get into rapport with people. If you get on with someone, you'll be in rapport with them. If you're not in rapport, there's probably a reason for that and you should pay attention to what it is.

If you think of rapport as a barometer of a relationship, rather than something separate to it, then you'll probably get better results.

It's worth having a play with rapport, and paying particular attention to the way that it influences communication. If you're out shopping and you see someone selling something like double glazing, stop and watch - from a safe distance! Watch how the level of rapport influences the conversation and shows you how good a job the sales person is doing. In particular, watch the intricate dance that ensues when a sales person is trying to match the body posture of a customer who doesn't want to be matched.

For you to be interested in NLP, you may already think of yourself as a "people watcher". Well, don't just watch, watch and learn! Notice patterns, sequences and connections in relationships and - most importantly - put what you've learned into practice.

Plan your planning

I'm going to tell you what really effective communicators do to make their listeners sit up and pay attention. I'm going to tell you what they do to ensure their listeners respond as they are intended to. And you'll be surprised at how obvious it is.

Really effective communicators plan their communication.

That's it? Yes, but that doesn't mean that they sit down and write a script, it means they tell their audience what they are supposed to do with the communication. Here's an example. I'm going to ask you a question. In a moment, I want you to make a choice. Here's something you need to decide on. You may have found that paragraph a little confusing, as it directed your attention in many different directions without closing any of the opening statements.

Before you say what you want to say, tell your audience what you want them to do. This is really just another way of directing people's attention, and it's very effective for managing the way people respond to what you say.

Here are a few more examples of this simple yet effective tool:

"I'm going to ask you a question now that I want you to think very carefully about before you answer"

"In a moment, I'm going to ask you to stand up"

"Here's a really important point for you to consider"

"This is what I want you to do"

"Before you fill out your feedback forms, I'm going to ask you a question"

"When we get back from lunch, I'm going to have you do some really creative group work"

"Before you finish reading your handbook, I would like you to think of at least three new ways you'll use all the great stuff you're learning."

If you tie this simple concept in with the goal setting exercises that you'll read about later on, you will quickly become a very powerful and congruent communicator, because the people you speak to will be able to understand easily and quickly what you want from them. It may be agreement, it may be an answer, or it may just be their attention. Whatever you want, you're more likely to get it if you tell people what it is!

In organisations, people often launch into transmission mode during meetings and then wonder why their colleagues pull their project updates apart. Sometimes, decisions go round in circles forever and never quite get made. We have come to learn what to expect from meetings, and if you are invited to a meeting then there may be an implicit expectation that you'll contribute. Meetings everywhere would be far more productive if people applied this simple principle. For example, saying "Here is an update on my project, I don't need any advice or feedback at this stage, it's for your information only" tells people exactly what is expected of them. Conversely, presenting a huge volume of facts and figures and only then asking people to make a decision is simply asking for trouble. If you tell people up front what you expect, they will pay attention in the right places and be able to make a decision when you need them to, instead of saying they need more time to think.

So, this is what I'm asking you to do. Whenever you want a specific response to what you tell people, first tell them what you want them to do.

How to learn, in four easy lessons

Often, people who are experienced at something are called upon to train people who are inexperienced. This is often a terrible idea, for a very simple reason.

Whenever we learn something new, particularly a physical task, we go through four well known stages. I've often read descriptions of them, but no one has ever explained why they are so important for knowledge transfer before. Here are those four stages:

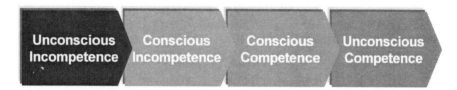

So, when learning a new skill you start by not even knowing that you can't do it, because you don't know it exists to be done. Then, you realise that you can't do it. As you start to learn it, you know that you can do it and you have to concentrate to do it well. Finally, the skill becomes deeply embedded and you can do it well without thinking about it. Think back to when you learned to ride a bicycle or drive a car and think about how you progressed through these stages.

 People who are skilled at a certain task are often the worst people to train others to perform that task. They have become unconsciously competent so they are only able to pass on the information that they have conscious access to, which is only part of the knowledge required for the task or skill. As a minimum, someone who is trained to model the skill and then structure the learning experience should facilitate this situation.

Did your father, or another friend or relative, try to teach you to drive? Was it the same as having a proper driving instructor? Many experienced drivers have forgotten how they learned to drive, so they try to describe what they are doing. This is not the same as describing how they are thinking.

By describing how they drive, they are offering a very limited part of their already limited representation of the world. They are often very good at telling the learner what not to do but are less able to identify what should be done instead.

Of course, not all professional driving instructors are perfect, but their focus is on learning to drive, not knowing how to drive. By focussing on the transition from not knowing to knowing they are able to convey that information more effectively than someone who knows how to drive, but doesn't know how they know.

Humans are very flexible and adaptable and are able to learn many more skills than they need to complete any given task. They always have more knowledge than is necessary and they are therefore able to improvise or respond to changes easily. The people in your audience will always have more relevant experience than they give themselves credit for, and you can exploit this to your advantage. By drawing out what is already within them, you will be blamed for their transformational learning experiences. You don't need to be an expert in the course material, just an expert in curiosity.

I suspect that you already know this, and that you already draw on learners' experiences a great deal. The key here is that your learners not only know more than you might think, they actually know a great deal more than they think because they just don't have conscious access to the majority of what they "know". When you start to hear those hallmark phrases that reveal a talent, such as "I don't know, I just do it" or "Doesn't everyone do that?" then spend a little time digging deeper, as you are about to hit gold.

Perhaps you remember sets and Venn diagrams from school. Set theory is a way of categorising elements into groups to make logical calculations easier.

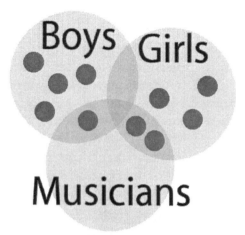

Here, you can see that two girls are musicians and three aren't. One boy is a musician and four aren't. Not surprisingly, there are no musicians that are both a girl and a boy and there are no musicians that are neither a girl nor a boy. This is a visual representation of a series of logical expressions which include:

Boy AND Musician = 1
Girl AND Musician = 2
Girl OR Musician = 5
Boy OR Girl = 10
Boy AND Girl = 0

Which is easier for you to understand? If you just want a single piece of information, it might be easier to read it from a table or spreadsheet. If you want to see the whole situation, the big picture, then the diagram might be easier. Different methods of coding information are useful at different times and for different purposes. Human spoken language is one way of coding information, but it's not the only one.

Here's a way of visually coding hierarchies of information:

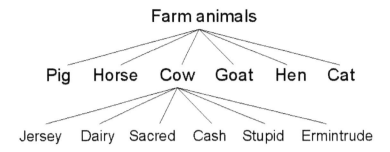

You can see that "cow" falls into the category "farm animals" and that "Jersey" falls into the category "cow". I'm afraid I'm not an expert on cows so some of them may not be farm animals in the strictest sense.

As you might expect, someone used this logical approach to categorise language too. Whenever we make statements about ourselves, our beliefs, our values, our rules and our needs we use language that falls neatly into levels of abstraction.

With language that relates to ourselves, the categories are:

Identity	Me, who I am
Beliefs	What is true about the world, my values, my rules
Capabilities	What I can do, everything that I know about
Behaviour	What I am doing right now
Environment	Where I am, the people around me, the world I live in

Here's another example, using the language of "limiting beliefs". Limiting beliefs are things that will hold you back and prevent you from succeeding, and the only thing that makes them true is that you believe they're true.

Identity	I'm not a teacher
Beliefs	I could never be a really good teacher
Capabilities	I can't teach
Behaviour	I'm not going to teach
Environment	I'm not teaching those people

If we turn the above examples into positive statements, we get:

Identity   I'm a teacher
Beliefs   I could be a really good teacher
Capabilities I can teach
Behaviour   I'm going to teach
Environment   I'll be teaching these people

Remember, positive doesn't mean good, it just means something that exists or is not negated.

When you want to communicate effectively with someone, especially in a facilitation or conflict situation, you will get better results by using your knowledge of logical levels. If someone says "I can't do this" then you can choose to stay at the same level (Yes you can, what *can* you do?) or you can move up a level (I know you will be able to do it) or down a level (What are you doing now?)

By identifying the logical level in language, you are able to determine how a person is structuring their thinking.

Here's a recent example from a NLP Practitioner course. On the subject of goals, one delegate said that her goal is "I want to be able to paint". Notice how this differs from "I want to paint" or "I want to paint people". She is asking for the skill, the capability - she may not actually do any painting. Of course, we can say that she already can paint, it just doesn't turn out how she'd like it to. You can use this structure to understand and clarify the problem, so that you're working at the most appropriate level to effect change.

When people talk about problems and in particular when they talk about things they can't do, you can use your knowledge of logical levels to either constrain their thinking within the problem or open their mind up to generate new ideas. Remember, if you address the stated problem directly you are saying, "Yes, I agree that you have this problem". In fact, that's so important I think we'll have a box:

 If you address the stated problem directly you are acknowledging and accepting the problem as real. Always move to a more useful position first before looking back to the problem if you need to. Many problems will disappear immediately as a result of directing your thoughts to the desired outcome. Any lingering problems are much easier to handle from a position of knowing the problem can be solved.

For example, if someone says "I want to be able to paint" and you respond with "How have you tried to learn?" then you are non-verbally saying, "You're right. You can't paint". A more useful response might be "So when you paint now, how does it look?" Oddly enough, this person had a particular problem with visualisation, so it's no wonder that she couldn't see her internal pictures clearly enough to transfer them onto paper. By the way, that's effectively what creative drawing is. You imagine a picture on the paper, and then you draw round it with a pencil.

If you choose to remain at the same level, you will constrain your thoughts within the problem. You will probably not generate any new ideas at this level, as the problem itself sets the boundaries for the solution. However, you may want this to happen, so it may not be a bad thing.

If you move up a level, you are able to think about other examples of this problem, and you will have better access to similar experiences to draw from. You will have better access to your skills by moving to a higher level than the problem.

If you move down a level, you will move from thinking to doing, you will increase the chances of taking action. You will start to motivate other people to take action.

Here are some examples of questions you can use to clarify problem statements:

"I'm not a xyz"	"What *are* you, then?"
"I'm not a xyz"	"What *can* someone who isn't a xyz do?"
"I'm no good at this"	"What *are* you good at?"
"I'm no good at this"	"What sort of person *would* be?"
"I'm no good at this"	"What *else* can you do?"
"I can't learn this"	"What makes you say that?"
"I can't learn this"	"What *are* you learning?"
"I can't learn this"	"What *can* you learn?"
"I'm not doing that"	"What *can* you do?"
"I'm not doing that"	"What *will* you do?"
"I'm not doing that"	"Where *could* you do that?"
"I'm not doing that here"	"Where *will* you do it?"
"I'm not doing that here"	"What *will* you do here?"

It's no coincidence that every response to these examples is a question. Remember, the person speaking these phrases is operating from an incomplete map of the world. They do not have an internal representation of the world that is complete - and neither do you!

This can come as a surprise to many people who have built their reputation on being right and on knowing everything. This is not a sign of arrogance or self-importance, it is merely a reflection of the situation that society puts trainers and teachers into. As a trainer, you are expected to have all the answers when it is generally more useful to have all the questions.

So, historically, the job of a teacher is to pass his or her map on to others. Fortunately for us, the role of the teacher or trainer is changing and becoming more like a facilitator or coach, helping students to learn for themselves.

So, your job is not to give the complete map to them, as you are only giving them your map and that is only useful to you. Your job is to help them recover the missing pieces of their own map. Consider, using each of the questions above, how the likely answers differ to what would happen if you just said "why not?"

 You will not help people by giving them your internal map, as it is only useful to you. Your job is to help them enrich their own map, and the way to do that is to ask them questions about the missing pieces.

Since you have no way to know how someone else structures their experience of the world, you have no way of knowing what parts are missing from their map. What may seem like missing information may in fact be a different way of organising that information to you. You may have experienced talking to someone who "just won't be told" and now you know why!

We'll leave logical levels in peace for now, as they will pop up again later on.

Maps

Language represents a tiny part of the experience that every person has in their head. Language does not convey experience – it summarises it. When someone makes a statement like "I can't learn this", you can ask yourself "what must their experience be, in order for this statement to be true".

 Often, people do or say things that don't make sense to you. Every behaviour makes complete sense for the person concerned. Your job is not to judge based on your map, it is to ask yourself "what must this person believe, think or need for this behaviour to be the best choice available?"

To understand someone, you must enter their world, not stand on the edge of your own and pass judgement.

By doing this, you are gaining a glimpse into their internal world. You must not be tempted to fill in the gaps you perceive in their experience. You must help them recover lost information themselves, not give it to them on a plate. If you responded to "I can't learn this" with "Yes you can, because other people are!" then you are giving them your experience, not helping them to expand their own.

Giving someone a piece of your map - "a piece of your mind" - is pointless as your map is incomplete too. In fact, they have bits that you don't so think of this situation as an opportunity to exchange ideas, not to give them.

It's very useful to realise that the more people you talk to about an event or experience, the more accurate your representation of it becomes - if you are willing to accept their version of events as true too.

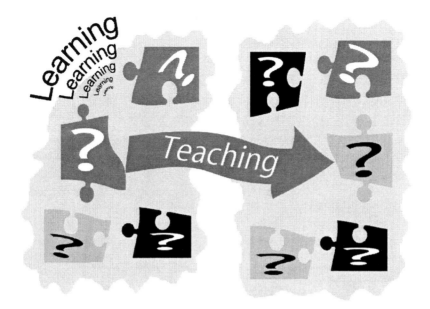

Giving a piece of your map is "teaching". Pointing to missing pieces encourages "learning". Choose which is more useful!

The interesting thing about truth is that some people often think it's mutually exclusive. IT ISN'T!! You can be right AND other people can be right too. Of course, being a reasonable person, you knew this already.

The more interpretations of the world that you build into your map of the world, the more complete and useful it will become. This won't happen if you continually judge other people's maps as being wrong because they're different to yours. After all, two different maps can't both be right can they?

Think of a street map of London and a tube map of London. Which is right? If one is right, the other must be wrong! Of course not, and by using both you get twice the useful information. Think of maps of experience in the same way and you'll find things much easier.

When someone is saying that they can't or won't do something, there are two amazingly simple yet effective questions that you can ask to change forever the way that they think about their problem. These questions are only known to the world's top secret change magicians, so you must promise to use them wisely.

These two magical questions are **"what stops you?"** and **"what would happen if you did?"**

No, you didn't miss anything. That's all there is to it.

Remember that you tend to get what you focus on. By asking people about their problem, you are focussing their attention squarely on the problem itself. The more they look at it, the bigger it gets. Throw in some well meaning counselling or therapy and the problem will soon be big enough to be insurmountable.

"Tell me about it"..."Oh dear"..."Why?"..."Why not?"...These questions just embed the problem deeper.

The first question focuses attention on the nature of the problem – what properties the problem has that cause it to hinder progress. The question puts the person back in control of the problem and separates them from it. They are able to explore the problem as a temporary barrier as the important word in the question is "stop" which implies that time is no longer passing. When people talk about problems, they are often referring to things that happened in the past as if they are happening through the present and future. By asking, "what stops you", you are freezing the problem in time and preventing it from affecting the future which is, of course, unwritten.

A sneaky variation on this is "how do you stop yourself?"

The second question focuses attention on the future after the problem has been solved. It is similar to asking "do you need the problem" but that is often too abstract to be useful. Asking "what would happen if you did" forces the person to create an internal experience of the future in which he or she has moved past the current limitation or barrier. In order to answer the question, the person must create this new future representation. In order to create that representation, a very important change must happen inside the person's head. Their world now contains the possibility that there is a solution to the problem. If they can imagine it, then it can exist.

When someone says "I can't learn this" and you ask "what stops you?" they will tell you what barriers exist in their perception of the world. You can now work on these barriers directly and remove them, move them aside or lower them – whatever metaphor works for the person in question. You don't even have to work on the barrier itself in most cases, so you don't have to spend time "solving" the problem. You can just ask them to move it aside for a moment and, if they still need it, they can move it back again afterwards. Since the person imposes these barriers, the person can move them too. If you listen to their language and watch the way they gesture when they talk, you'll see them describe the barrier and tell you where it is. You can either move it yourself, or you can get them to move it. If you just go right ahead and work on the assumption that they can do whatever they're having difficulty with, you'll find that the barrier disappears by itself in most cases.

When someone says, "I can't learn this" and you ask, "what would happen if you did?" they have to create an internal representation of themselves having learned whatever they can't learn. The possibility now exists that the subject is learnable by them, given time and resources. The barrier is now gone!

In contrast, if you respond with "why not?" then you accept their model of the world and the limitation that exists within it. You are effectively saying, "Yes, I agree that you can't learn this. Now justify yourself". In return, they will do just that – they will give you a list of very plausible reasons that support their limiting belief. In fact, every time you ask "why not?" they will convince themselves, and you, a little more.

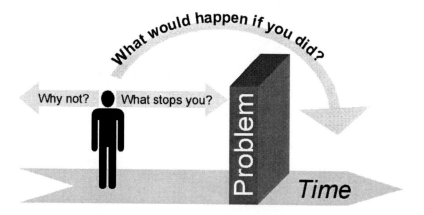

This process of recovering lost information is very relevant to Logical Levels too. If, when you are explaining something, you jump levels, you are demanding that your audience makes a leap of logic to fill in the missing levels. A nice, smooth progression through levels guides the listener's brain on a journey. They will pay more attention to you because they are not 'inside' creating missing information and they will find information easier to absorb and learn.

When explaining a new idea or concept, the name that you give this idea is expressed as an Identity level statement. A smooth progression through levels would be something like this:

The name of the concept
What it is good for
What it can do
An example of how you might use it
When and where you would use it

If you are the kind of trainer who likes to build knowledge up rather than start with abstract theories and work down, then this might suit you better:

A situation you might find yourself in
What you would normally do in that situation
All the things that you could do in that situation
What is true to say about that situation
A name for the concept or idea

Of course, in order to fully communicate with your audience, you would use both to appeal to different learning styles. Here's an example.

NLP is a personal development toolkit that can be applied to personal change, problem solving and a great many other situations. In training, you might use NLP to communicate effectively with your audience during a part of your training course where you want them to remember information easily.

If you're in a situation where you want to explain the connection between language and behaviour, you might start by running through the whole list of profiling categories, giving examples of language and behaviour. You could ask the delegates to explain it to each other, or you could ask them to read the list of categories and work through a written example. In any case, what's important is that they start to hear the patterns in normal speech and correlate them to behavioural choices. Then, when they have some real experience to build on they can understand the relevance of the name 'metaprograms'.

Hopefully, you noticed that the two last paragraphs were an example of this smooth progression idea. In the first half, the Identity level label was 'NLP' and in the second half it was 'metaprograms'.

"Metaprogram" is NLP jargon for a category of personality trait that can be recognised in language and behaviour. Metaprograms perform the same basic function as any other profiling method in that by listening to language structures you can predict behavioural tendencies. Also, by tuning your language to that native to a person's particular metaprograms, you will communicate easily and effectively.

The one big advantage of NLP metaprograms over other profiling methods is that you don't need to fill in forms or questionnaires - you can profile someone whilst having a normal conversation. Once you start to hear how the structure of language is littered with the debris of mental processes you'll wonder how you didn't hear these patterns before.

In order for a person's natural language to shift from one level to another - from "I know how to drive" to "I'm a good driver", for example - specific internal processes take place. We have names for most of these processes, for example, if someone shifts from talking about what she can do to what she is doing then we might call that either motivation, or making a decision, depending on the context. If someone shifts from talking about what they are doing to what they can do, then they have moved from conscious competence to unconscious competence - a process that we might call mastering a skill.

You can hear these shifts in language patterns as you take people through a learning experience. They are a very important indicator to you that your learners are rearranging their internal organisation to integrate what you are helping them to learn. They are adding new information to their maps of the world.

Of course, not only your audience's language can shift during a learning experience - yours can too. You can intentionally shift language patterns at specific points in time to effect change in your audience.

You can think of motivation as being the mental process that takes place when a person naturally moves from thinking at the Capability level to thinking at the Behaviour level. Therefore, by changing the structure of your language you can directly influence people to take action.

By listening to how people talk, you can understand how they think. The reverse is also true, so people will switch thinking modes depending on how you talk.

When you listen to people talking about skills, tasks, learning and abilities you will hear a number of interesting language structures that give you a great deal of useful information about what they have learned.

When you hear "I can" or "I can't" you know that the person is talking about capabilities. When you hear "I do" or "I don't" you know that they are talking about behaviour. The two are fundamentally different and must not be confused or generalised to the same meaning.

Language itself is a generalised, distorted, filtered metaphor of what is really happening inside your head.

Here are some examples of the kinds of statements you will hear from learners, along with a translation that recovers the original thinking. Read the antidotes carefully as some may look the same but are slightly different.

	Meaning	Antidote
Can	I have the ability and knowledge to do this	Good! (How did you learn?)
Can not	I am imagining this being done, I do not yet know how to do this myself	What would happen if you did? What stops you?
Will	I have both the ability and the intention/motivation to do this	Good! (How did you decide?)
Will not	I have the ability to do this but not the intention/motivation	What would help you decide to do this?
Could	I have the ability to do this but execution is conditional on another factor	What stops you? What would happen if you did?
Could not	I am imagining this being done, I imagine myself trying and failing	What stops you? What would it be like if you could?
Would	I have the ability to do this but something is stopping me	How do you stop yourself? What would happen if you did?
Would not	I have the ability to do this but an internal value or belief is stopping me	How do you stop yourself? What would happen if you did?

Might	I have the ability to do this but have not yet decided whether to or not	How will you choose? How will you know?
Might not	I have the ability to do this and probably will although I want to retain free choice	How might you stop yourself?
Do	I regularly do this or am doing this 'now'	Good! (How did you learn?)
Do not	My internal values or beliefs prevent me from doing this or even thinking about doing it	How did you decide not to? Was there a time when you did?
Am	I place myself in the category of...	What kind of things does that enable you to do?
Am not	I place myself outside of the category of...	What are you then? What kind of things does that enable you to do?

The word "now" has a special meaning in relation to language. Essentially "now" doesn't necessarily mean this present moment, which was just then anyway. "Now" means an ongoing period of time that you internally think of as the present. For some people, "now" means anytime between last week and next week. For others, "now" is just a few minutes long. Some people even have a period of "now" that lasts for years. Everything that happens within this moving window of time is happening "now" so you might say "I'm going to the gym again now" or "I'm working in London now". It doesn't mean that you are there right at this moment, it means "in the present" or "these days".

I know you already knew that, but I wanted to point it out because it's one of those simple things that we take for granted that reveal huge amounts of useful information. You know that I'm writing this now, but that's a different now from the now when you're reading this. I'm writing this now, and you're reading this now. We are connected through time and space by these words. In fact, we are all connected through time and space by the words we use.

It's always interesting to recognise the many ways that people differ, and the range of possibilities that exist within our perception of experience. Time itself is highly subjective and different people will think of time in different ways. In particular, what one person calls a short wait is an eternity for someone else.

As you start to hear the way that language reveals the structure of experience, you will hear many different ways that people organise their internal resources. The more you listen, the more amazed you'll be at the differences between our maps of the world, and the better you'll be at communicating effectively with other people.

Paying attention

Although this isn't strictly anything to do with training (or maybe it is) and it's not strictly NLP (in that you wouldn't see it in a course manual) it actually demonstrates one of the key principles that underpin NLP. Without understanding this, people who complete NLP courses just go around doing NLP to people instead of really absorbing and integrating it. Maybe you've met people like that in the past - I have, and they certainly put me off NLP!

Many years ago, I had a proper job as a telecoms engineer. I remember when I was an apprentice, young and impetuous and with a talent for problem solving. I really could understand complex systems very easily, although sometimes I started taking the thing apart before stopping to find out what was actually wrong with it. I really believe that my formal training in systemic problem solving was a real asset to the work that I do now. Anyway, one day I went to a factory in the West Midlands with the local engineer to fix a telephone. I went straight to the telephone, picked it up and started taking the back off with my screwdriver. The engineer stopped me and suggested I just pick up the handset and listen instead of diving straight in. What I heard wasn't dial tone, but the kind of sound you'd hear if a button were pressed down. Just by stopping and listening, I heard everything I needed to know to solve the problem.

A few years later I went to a big tyre factory in Stoke on Trent to carry out a software upgrade on a piece of equipment. I waited until everyone had gone home, and then set to work. The upgrade should have taken less than an hour but half way through the equipment developed a fault. I spent a few hours trying to fix it, and then drove back to Telford to pick up a spare, and then back to Stoke. I finally gave up at about one o'clock in the morning. The next morning, I met my manager on site and immediately set to work on the equipment again. He stopped me and suggested that I just stand in front of the equipment rack and watch. I didn't see anything helpful, so he suggested I pay attention to the lights on the front.

These things have lights just like the ones on your car's dashboard, telling you what the status of the system is. This piece of equipment had two circuit boards which were physically identical apart from the position of a switch that told the system that either Telex terminals or Telex lines were attached. On the back of the equipment, terminals or lines would be physically plugged in. In this case, there were 7 terminals and 2 lines, so on the terminal card there were 7 lights and on the line card, 2 lights.

So, as I watched, I began to notice that the system was telling me it had 7 lines and 2 terminals attached. Remember that switch? All I had done was take the two cards out then put them back in the wrong slots. That was it, and all I had to do was watch. On the other hand, I got 8 hours overtime, so it's not all bad news.

On a NLP Practitioner course recently, someone was trying to do an exercise called the "fast phobia cure" with her partner, who said he was afraid of cockroaches. She couldn't get the technique to work, so I asked him what he was afraid of. What he told me was that he lived in Spain for a while and one day he saw a cockroach in his kitchen that ran out from behind a chopping board. The cockroach surprised him, then sat, looking at him in an evil way. Now, as you know, cockroaches don't look evil. In fact, neither do people - words like "evil" or "happy" tell you that the person is adding some information on top of what they directly saw, heard or felt - they're adding some of their own experience. Now, if you really pay attention to what this person was saying, you can hear that he's not afraid of what the cockroach actually did - he's afraid of what he imagined that it might do. When we asked him to run through the actual experience, he wasn't scared at all. When we asked him to run through what he imagined might happen, the cockroach flew up into his face and attacked him. Who in their right minds wouldn't be afraid of that?

Here's another example - someone asked me to help him overcome his fear of public speaking. Now, you might jump to the conclusion that he was afraid of public speaking, so here's his original request for help, exactly as he said it.

"I would like to be able to accept invitations to speak publicly as easily as you did".

So, what does that tell you he's afraid of? Public speaking? No! He loves that bit! In fact, he's afraid of accepting. So, what happens between accepting and presenting? He worries. He's afraid of worrying. When he gets to do the presentation, he loves it - he gets a buzz out of it. Then he says to himself "I wish I could remember the feeling of the buzz for next time", so that was exactly what I had him do.

In problem solving, people will tell you the exact nature of the problem, and give you the solution, within the first sentence or so, as long as you pay attention to what's really there instead of inserting your own experience or expectations.

So, you won't find that in any NLP book that's based only on the visible techniques of NLP. A book like this, that lets you soak up the attitude and approach of NLP is full of stories that help you to learn what's really important.

Remember - if you don't have the mindset right, the techniques will never work. If you have the right mindset, the techniques will come naturally. It's easy to write down techniques, it's not so easy to help people learn an attitude. For this, we need a highly advanced, highly efficient and highly overlooked form of communication - the story.

Time is very important for all sorts of reasons and since we've already mentioned the concept of "now" we may as well spend some more time on the subject.

Time is subjective. This means that every person thinks of time differently. We all have a shared hallucination of the passage of time that is indicated by clocks, but two people in the same room at the same time, looking at the clock and seeing the same time will have different perceptions of time flying or dragging, depending on their focus of attention.

Someone who is totally focussed and enthralled will think that time has flown. Someone who is thinking of other things will be clock watching and will perceive time passing at a crawl.

What makes the difference? Well, partly it's to do with the way that your ability to absorb information is controlled by a part of your brain called the Reticular Activating System. This information is of no use to you unless you have your electrodes handy. What is more useful is to know that you tend to get more of what you focus on. Focussing on boredom will therefore make you more bored. There's certainly a connection between being bored and being boring, as proven by the

Pet Shop Boys. I don't mean that they're boring, I'm just reminding you that they sang about it. You may think they're boring which is entirely up to you.

You can use a number of methods to direct someone's attention, and the first we'll talk about is engaging whatever is being focussed on and using it to draw in the listener. A very powerful way to engage attention is with stories. Stories encourage the brain to create internal representations, which, surprisingly enough, are what memories and facts and figures are.

Later on, you'll learn about the brain being an analogue computer. Don't learn about it now, just forget I mentioned it. Go on, really try to forget it.

Are you starting to get the idea of how to focus attention? Anyway, since the brain is an analogue computer it cannot directly represent anything that doesn't exist. This includes anything which is somewhere else, any time other than now and involving any person other than you. Why do you think you identify with characters in films or songs? Because they're YOU!

So, if you tell a story about someone who lived a long time ago in a faraway land who was really, really excited at the thought of being able to learn really easily then your brain can only make sense of the information by transporting you to that land and time and into the mind of that person.

I knew someone once who was very inquisitive and always wanted to know how things worked. As the years went by, this person stopped wondering how things worked and turned his attention to how people worked. You know what it's like, to watch someone and wonder what goes on between their ears. Sometimes, you watch someone and wonder if anything at all goes on between their ears! Anyway, one day this person found herself sitting and reading a book that answered all the questions that he had had and giving her insight into all those curious things that went on in the world. Now, it doesn't always matter too much what the exact detail of the book was. I forget anyway. Time's like that - things that you're really certain about one day become a bit fuzzy the day after. Soon you can't quite remember what you were certain about all those years ago and once again your mind becomes open to new ideas because certainty is a sign that your mind has pulled down the shutters and that's the last thing you wanted, wasn't it?

Stories are a very powerful way of communicating directly with each person in a large audience. Why? Well, in order to make sense of a story, the listener identifies with the story, searching for relevance and connecting their own experience with that of the characters in the story. Therefore, your story will connect with the unique experience in each listener's mind, creating a totally new story that involves the listener at a very personal and relevant level. If you tell a story to 30 people, you'll end up with 31 stories.

Everyone loves a story. You can call it an anecdote, gossip, a tale, a rumour, a case study, a report or anything else you like that makes it acceptable, respectable or true. Some people have a problem with the word story because it implies that the information is made up or untrue. Sometimes this is the case and sometimes it isn't and that's not relevant to the structure of the story or its effect on the listener.

If you believe in truth then consider this - how do you know that the news is true? You can read two newspaper accounts of the same event and read two totally different stories because of different political affiliations. You already know that the truth can be bent, but how far will it bend before it becomes a lie? That is entirely subjective and depends on your point of view. If you're a Star Wars fan you'll recall that Obi Wan Kenobi told Luke Skywalker that his father was dead. When Luke found out that his father was very much alive and living as Darth Vader, he thought that Obi Wan had lied to him. It turned out that Obi Wan had used the term "dead" metaphorically, which made it all right. Language is such a collection of metaphor and distortion that it's hard enough to be precise, let alone true.

So, if you want stories to be true, use true stories. If you don't mind either way then let your imagination run riot. Years ago when I was a service engineer (yes, I had a proper job once) I used to visit a large international bank where there was a big room full of people sending and receiving Telex messages. This was the first job for many people joining the bank from school and at the end of the room, behind a desk, sat the supervisor. Breaks were strictly policed and at lunchtime the whole room closed down. I remember on a few occasions walking in to that room at lunchtime. Do you think the room was empty, all these young bankers down the pub or enjoying a frolic in the park? (The room had no windows!) Well, every day, all the young Telex operators would bring their chairs down to the end of the room and sit and listen to stories. Every day, the supervisor would tell stories about how life used to be in the bank, about the people that had been and gone and about her own journey through the ranks. Every day, the audience would sit in a hushed and reverent silence until lunchtime was over and they would shuffle back to their terminals.

Now, if you had told them that they weren't allowed to leave the room at lunchtime, what would have happened?

Time can easily be distorted and used to suspend an audience's perception of 'real' time - whatever that is.

Here's a really simple way of moving people, internally, back to another time. Start off talking about past events using past tense for your verbs. The easy way to do this is just to imagine that "now" is the present moment and that you are looking back to the past. Your language will naturally reflect this.

When you notice your audience doing things like staring into the distance or to one side, shift your verb tense to the present. Again, you just imagine that you have stepped back in time and that "now" is in fact "back then". Here's an example.

Do you remember your first day at school? What was it like? Do you remember the sights, sounds, maybe you remember the taste or smell of school dinners? Perhaps you can imagine what the layout of the school was like for you back then, the rooms, the hall, the playground. I don't know if you can imagine it really clearly but as you look around you and just soak up the sounds, what is the first thing that you notice? Do you see a teacher? Does everything seem bigger? Do you hear those sounds of children playing outside? Do you remember the summer of your exams? Can you hear the calls of the children outside in the sunshine as you sit in the examination room? Maybe the smell of the freshly cut playing field wafts in through a window? Maybe particular people spring to mind? Friends? Teachers? Dinner ladies? Well, you can enjoy it for as long as you like before you return to the present time.

After you have read through that paragraph, go back through and notice the verb tenses. Notice how they shift from past to present just before half way. Imagine how different a History lesson would be if you were really there. The great thing about this is that everyone listening gets drawn in to their own personal version of the story.

Did you know that Roman soldiers used to drink vinegar when they were marching? I don't know if that's the same kind of vinegar that they have at the chip shop, or if it's something like my Dad's home made wine that just used to taste like vinegar but you can imagine how you feel on a really hot, dry day when you've been running around or walking a long way and you can imagine sitting down under a shady tree with your Roman friends and taking a long, refreshing drink of….lovely warm vinegar…. Maybe not.

Anyway, the point is that our perception of 'the time' and of the flow of time is subjective, changes from one moment to the next and can be influenced by the simple use of language. Language is a digital system used to encode analogue information, so, just like in your CD player at home, the end result is not exactly what you started with but it's usually close enough. Yes, all audio recording systems lose information. The telephone network carries only a tiny part of the frequency range that we use in human speech. We can cope with this loss because we are able to rebuild the lost information based on our experience. The richness of experience that is lost in the translation from thought to speech is far greater and, unfortunately, when we rebuild the lost information, the end result is never what was intended, and I use the word "never" with caution.

A digital system like language can represent things that aren't here and now but your analogue brain can only process this information within a framework of "here, now, me". This is also why instructions starting with the word "Don't..." often get the opposite result to what you intend. More on this later. Don't think about it just yet.

Some words are stories in themselves in that they represent a complex collection of memories - sounds, images, feelings, tastes and smells. In order for your brain to process any language, words are converted into basic sensory representations. In fact, every word is a metaphor in that the word itself is not the object or idea described, it is only a label for it.

Every word in every language is a metaphor. A word is not the thing it describes; it is only a label for it. To process any word, your brain converts it into a basic sensory representation. Therefore, all language has the same effect as telling a story, to a degree.

So you can't eat the word apple, but you know what an apple is. How about rich, dark, moist chocolate fudge cake on a white china plate, with warm chocolate fudge oozing out of it, topped off with a big dollop of cheese? Your words have more emotional impact when the listener can engage their internal senses and become fully associated with what you are describing - as if it is really happening to them.

It's important to realise that people choose words because they represent the internal sensory experience that's going on. If you're running a workshop and you're summarising comments on a whiteboard, you may be tempted to translate, summarise or rephrase in order to write the comments down. You should only do this if your intention is to confuse and frustrate the audience, demonstrating to them that you are paying no attention to their ideas.

Think of the most indulgent and delicious pudding or dessert you every had in your life. Describe it to me. Now let me write on the whiteboard "cake". Does that do it justice?

Asking people to give you synonyms for words that you suspect to be vague is a good way to uncover the experience represented by the word. For example, if you ask people for a synonym for "professionalism" you will get answers ranging from "looks smart" through "honest" and on to "confident" and "expert".

For years, presentation and business communication courses taught that in order to demonstrate understanding, we have to paraphrase and restate. NO! This demonstrates that you understand your version, not that you understand the other person. If you really want to demonstrate understanding, repeat back the key words verbatim.

Paraphrasing demonstrates that you are representing someone else's memories by converting them into your own.

Repeating key words verbatim demonstrates that you are respecting someone else's memories.

Choose which outcome you want before deciding whether to rephrase or repeat.

Some words are far richer than others. A word like "apple" means something different to everyone, in that everyone will think of a different apple. However, when we see an apple, we all use the same label for it so whilst it's still a generalisation, it's vague enough to be OK. When a course delegate describes an apple and you write "apple" on the whiteboard, everyone will know what you mean, even though everyone will translate the word into a different internal sensory representation (i.e. a different apple).

If a delegate describes a situation where people sometimes arrive in the office late, you might write the word "unprofessional" on the whiteboard. Maybe you've done something like this in the past, and experienced first hand the disagreement and confusion that it leads to. When people are disagreeing in this situation, they are not arguing over the word, they are arguing over their internal representations. If you try to condense every suggestion and find a single, unifying word, you will be standing at the whiteboard all day, unless you summarise every suggestion and write only the words "important things" on the whiteboard.

There's a simple reason for this complex problem. People are arguing because they are talking about completely different memories and experiences to that originally described. Everyone has an experience of people being late for work. Some people get really upset about it whilst others don't even care. Even though they are talking "in general", they are describing specific events in their personal history. They are telling you about their beliefs and values. You will never, ever reach an agreement because everyone is talking about a different experience through different perceptual filters.

If you have to, write 30 different words for "being late" on the whiteboard until you have successfully captured each individual memory. You may even stand back in amazement, never before having realised that people could see things so differently. The delegates may be amazed too, and may even start to develop a respect for each other's beliefs and language. You will only achieve this if you respect the words that people use.

If your intention is to create a single, common representation then I still don't advise you use the bulldozer of paraphrasing as you are only using synonyms that make sense to you. There are far better ways of gaining collective agreement, and here are three of them.

Go up

Take all of the different suggestions and find the level at which they unify. Take "arriving late at the office" and ask, "what is that an example of" or "what is important about that". Sooner or later you will end up with a collective agreement that "respecting the value of your colleagues" is important, even though being early or late is down to individual preference. You may well find that "professionalism" is important to everyone, but the difference is the process by which you arrived at that word.

Instead of saying, "Punctuality equals professionalism" you are saying, "Punctuality is an example of professionalism" which is very different. If you go back to the chapter on logical levels, the first example here is like saying "a pig is a cow" whereas the second example is more like "pigs and cows both live on farms". One respects people's maps of the world, the other doesn't. You decide which to use.

Start again

If you can't agree on a representation, make up a new one. For example, what is the best state to be in to deliver a presentation? You may get lots of different replies including "relaxed", "objective", "confident" and "knowledgeable" in which case you could make up a new state called ROCK, which allows each person to integrate their own beliefs with some new ideas that they've picked up.

Use brute force

What if two people disagree over ideas that are exact opposites? Well, with all of these things I suggest you cheat. This is a special form of cheating that appears to everyone else to be highly skilful but which you know is really easy. Let's say one person says you should be confident and the other says you should be nervous. The word "should" tells you that they are comparing what is being suggested to their internal set of rules and values. You "should" be confident because their rules say so.

Again, you can handle this in many different ways, and here are two suggestions.

First, you can say, "I can see that you both strongly agree with each other that your state of mental preparation is very important", so you force them into an agreement. In fact, they are agreeing with other if you look at the situation from a certain level. If I say red and you say blue, we both agree that colour is important and we both care intensely about making the right choice. We're just arguing over detail.

Second, you can say, "Would it be most useful to be confidently nervous or nervously confident?" Not possible, but useful. You know that it's possible, and asking which is most useful creates a new state that encompasses the most positive aspects of the two original states. Even the most opposite views can be squashed together in this way because in order to make sense of the new suggestion, the brain must move up to a higher logical level where it is possible for the two states to co-exist.

What may look or sound like disagreement is in fact an agreement over necessity and a disagreement over detail.

Stories are a very powerful means of communication and you'll be surprised at how much factual, specific information can be conveyed more meaningfully and memorably by using a story. You've probably heard mnemonic stories for remembering sequences of data or components of a business process and these are certainly very useful as they engage more parts of the listener's brain than mere repetition of the list. The idea is that the learner goes for a walk in a park, or a shopping trip, or a day at the seaside, and along the journey sees things that link back to the sequence to be remembered. They key to using this successfully is to create a natural flow from one element to the next.

Which of these is easier to remember:

Red - Orange - Yellow - Green - Blue - Indigo - Violet

Richard of York Gave Battle In Vain

Our brains can recall huge amounts of information, but many people find sequencing that information difficult. Therefore, any format that can create a structured sequence around "raw" data can only be a useful thing.

I should finally add that every story in this book is absolutely and entirely true. Only the places, times and people involved may have changed during the editing process.

Did you forget that this chapter was about stories? Maybe I did too, or maybe life itself is just one long story...

Environment

Just a short word on the environment.

I've worked in many training centres, some of them converted from other buildings like hotels, many of them custom built training and conference centres.

One thing I've noticed that most of them have in common is that they are very carefully designed and built training centres. That does not make them learning centres.

The emphasis is on the trainer, not the learners. Rooms arranged like classrooms, fluorescent lighting, space at the front of the classroom for a desk and an OHP and a screen or whiteboard at the front of the room for everyone to sit and stare at.

So, if you have the opportunity to design a working environment, design it from the point of view of the people it is intended to serve, not the person who books it.

Think of the environments that make you feel most relaxed and receptive. Think of the places where you feel most safe and comfortable. Those are great learning states. Stress, anxiety, feeling self conscious – these are not learning states.

So, give some thought to these aspects of the environment:

What colours relax you and make you feel at home?

What kind of furniture lets you know you're either at home or at work?

What sounds let you know you can relax and that you are safe?

What words make you feel happy and relaxed?

How can you create a learning environment so that it looks, feels and sounds as little like a school as possible?

Memories are made of this...

You know how one little thing reminds you of a whole series of memories? Maybe a smell brings an entire holiday back, or a certain colour or sound reminds you of something special? In NLP jargon, these triggers are called Anchors.

Anchoring is a perfectly natural process that is part of your brain's memory storage system. By connecting sensory experiences with simple reference markers, an entire memory can be brought to life with one simple stimulus, like a certain smell takes you back to that holiday, or a certain piece of music brings to mind a vivid memory of someone special.

 How can you use this natural process to your own advantage? Here are a few ideas.

Preparing yourself for an important presentation, reprogramming phobias, as an accelerated learning tool, as a tool for focussing the attention of a group, for influencing behaviour, for relaxing yourself or other people, for getting yourself out of bed on Monday morning, for getting yourself to sleep on Monday night or just for making yourself feel great about dealing with life's distractions.

Advertisers know how this process works and they use it to connect a particular emotional state with their brand name and logo. If you watch commercials on TV, you'll notice that some of them seem to bear no relation to the product they're advertising. You'll see a series of images that have certain connotations, like security, happiness, love and desire and at the end of the advert you just see a brand name. You should pay attention to the music, as it's just as important as the images. One group of adverts that spring to mind are those for the Peugeot 406. The images were of great heroic acts, saving lives and being generally manly, whilst being caring and understated. The music was M People's "Search for the hero". There's no need to say what Peugeot wants its customers to think of themselves.

So, how does anchoring work? Well, you basically get yourself into a heightened emotional state – any one will do – and then see, hear or feel some unique, simple sensory stimulus such as a word, sound, image or touch. You could visualise a colour, hear a word, speak a word or squeeze your hand in a certain way – all of these work well as anchors and work best when used together.

Anchoring has always been a difficult process to describe in a book as your attention is on the book instead of your own state, so I've tried something different here. Have a go and see what you think.

Read through this following piece of text, only turning the page at the end when you have finished reading. As you reach the end of the text, pay attention to any feelings you have and then turn over the page.

It's probably a good idea to have the page ready to turn before you start reading so that you can catch the relaxed state while it lasts.

You may want to sit somewhere relatively quiet to do this.

Memories are made of this...   NLP - Skills for Learning

Imagine yourself lying in a warm meadow. You feel the warmth of the sun's rays on your skin and in your hair. A cool breeze whispers past the hairs on your skin like someone gently breathing your name.

You hear sounds, very quiet and distant and as you lie there with your eyes closed, you can just make out the distant music of birdsong. You realise that the birdsong is all around you, moving left and right, up and down. You open your eyes and see swallows darting through the crystal blue sky. Realising how bright and clear the Sun is, you take a deep breath, let your eyes gently close again and your attention drifts back to those sounds. You can hear the wind moving calmly through the trees and the sigh reminds you of the voice of someone special.

With the breeze drifting so lightly across the meadow, you reach out and feel how cool the grass is. The touch of the grass is so soothing on your hands that you press your palms into the grass and feel your fingers stretching right out as far as they can stretch.

As you hold your hands up to your face to shield your eyes from the brilliant Sun, you notice the smell of the grass on your hands and it reminds you of long summer evenings at home when the smell of fresh cut grass lingered in the air. Letting your mind wander through these wonderful memories for a while, your attention is slowly drawn back to the meadow as you realise that this is the most relaxed you have ever been in your life.

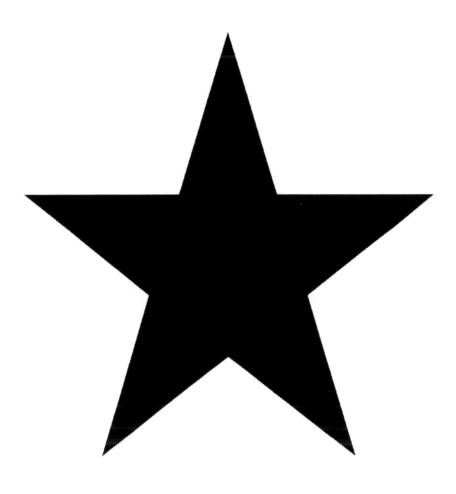

What do you think of that?

Now, you can wake yourself up and think about something else, maybe what you had for breakfast or what you'll do tonight. What colour is your favourite hat? Does a rainbow have red on the inside or the outside?

An important step in establishing an anchor is to break the anchored state and then return to it, so imagine yourself feeling really calm and tranquil and quickly look back at the star.

Now that the anchor is beginning to set, you can think of the last time you really laughed and the last film you saw.

Now, look back at the star again and notice what happens to your feelings of relaxation.

People naturally emphasise the things they say. They point in a certain direction whenever they talk about the future. They use a certain voice tone to indicate uncertainty. They touch you whenever they laugh. They install anchors in you, all day, every day. It's time you started fighting back!

In a learning environment, it can be very useful to create anchors for certain states that the audience could benefit from. There will naturally be times when the audience are curious, certain, happy or wide awake. There are some very long winded ways to get the audience into a receptive state, but you can already add up what you've read so far and achieve the same thing in about 30 seconds. On top of this, you can anchor the state and return to it instantly, any time you need to.

You might choose a certain word, or a visual symbol such as a toy or coloured pen to switch states. The important thing is consistency. When you see the audience move naturally into a certain state, grab it with an anchor. When they laugh, anchor it with a gesture, word, colour - anything you have to hand.

When the audience is in a focussed state, anchor it so that you can get people's attention back after exercises. When the audience is quiet at the start of the course, anchor their reluctance to speak and use it to control debates that are getting out of hand.

Is confusion a useful state to anchor?

You may be screaming "Oh no! This is manipulative" in which case don't do it. Just carry on doing this the way you already naturally do.

As you may already know, a lot of NLP is used in the area of influence and persuasion. This doesn't mean that NLP is inherently persuasive, it just means that in the course of developing NLP, some very influential and persuasive people were modelled. This issue always comes up on NLP training courses, so here's my view.

One of the keys to understanding how to benefit from NLP is to throw away your value judgements about behaviours and beliefs. Behaviour that you may label "wrong" is actually very effective in a different context. Someone once said on a training course that he wanted to stop shouting at his kids. I said, "Imagine for a moment that there is a miracle psychological tool that can remove from your brain the ability to shout at your kids. Life would be wonderful, you would never even be able to shout, let alone have to stop yourself, and your home life will be relaxing and enjoyable. One day, when you're in town with your kids, one of them steps into the road in front of a car……and you can't shout" As usual, the problem is actually just a symptom.

You can be quite certain that people had the ability to be manipulative, influential and persuasive long before NLP came along. You shouldn't give NLP more credit than it deserves!

Making an Impact

Really **impactful** communication takes place when you are delivering the same message with all of your communication systems - your words, your voice, your eyes, your hands, your breathing, your body posture, your movement and every thought that you have.

You can spend a lot of time trying to remember all of these different activities, or you can do it the easy way - and you know how much I like the easy way!

The easy way to be 'congruent' is to start by **believing what you are saying**. If your conscious and unconscious minds agree, you will send the same message through all of your communication systems. You don't have to remember all that body language stuff you read about years ago. It will all happen naturally and thereby be far more convincing.

If you've ever stood there, speaking to a group and not really wanting to be there, do you think it's enough to just say the words? No! They can tell! Audiences, like dogs, can smell fear.

Many people have written excellent books on how to focus your thoughts and clear your mind in order to be totally congruent. I won't rewrite them here, but I will give you a few handy tips that you can use right away without having to read another book.

What do you want?

It's very important that you are very, very clear about what it is that **you** want. In order to set your brain up to automatically achieve your goals for you, your goals must conform to certain rules.

It's just like making sure that a computer program conforms to the syntax of the programming language. If it doesn't, it might still run but the results may be unexpected.

Here are the rules for "well formed outcomes". Your goals must be:

Stated positively - as something you want, rather than something you don't want.

Congruent - You must not lose anything as a result of achieving this goal, otherwise you will sabotage your own attempts. This often happens when people try to give up smoking.

About you and totally under your control. It is no use having a goal like "to get promoted" because that is probably not entirely under your control. A better goal would be "to do everything that I can possibly do to position myself for my promotion".

Testable using sensory evidence. It is not enough to say that you aim "to successfully complete" something. What does successful completion look, sound and feel like? Lets say your aim is to write a training course manual. How will you know when it's finished? Will you see it, sitting printed and bound on your desk? Will you read it, noticing the words? Will you pick it up and feel its weight, or flick through the pages? Everything that you 'know' is a sensory experience, stored in your memory. To easily achieve a goal, you must have a specific and direct sensory test for it.

When you have adapted your goal to meet these criteria, you can test it using this simple set of four questions, which check the goal logically (as in real logic, not just common sense). Ask yourself each question and wait until you get an answer. You can write your answers down if it helps.

If I achieve this, what will I gain?
If I achieve this, what will I lose?
If I don't achieve this, what will I gain?
If I don't achieve this, what will I lose?

And finally, pay really close attention to any feelings that you get as you ask yourself this last question:

If I were offered this right now, would I take it?

If there is anything that you haven't considered, or if any part of you would object to this goal, you will get a definite reaction to that question.

Have a dream

When are you at your most confident? Is it when you try something new, or when you do something you know you can do easily?

First, remember four or five specific times when you used skills or abilities that you value highly and that you want to have easy access to.

Allow yourself to daydream into those memories. See everything that you saw, hear everything that you heard and feel everything that you felt - both touch and emotions. Take some time to remember the whole event in as much detail as you can.

Now run the whole event again from a different point of view. If you were talking to someone, watch the event from over their shoulder. Notice how you look, your facial expressions, notice your tone of voice. Watch the event again from other points in the room. Make a mental note of anything new you learn whilst running through these memories.

Next, do the same exercise again but this time daydream into the future. Think about how the room will look, the people, the sound of your voice. See things both as yourself and also from the audience's chair. Notice how confident you look and sound. Take as long as you need to fully imagine the whole experience. See the audience nodding and smiling.

Repeat this a couple of times so that it becomes very easy to imagine. Run through this new 'memory' whenever you get a quiet moment. Imagine everything going well. If anything gets in your way, you are able to easily overcome it.

Splash in the puddle

First, pick the emotional state you want - certainty, confidence, passion, etc. Then, stand about 2 feet in front of an imaginary puddle on the floor.

Notice how the puddle is made of a pure colour - pick any colour you like that makes sense for the emotional state that is in the puddle. Watch the puddle for just a moment and then, only when you're ready, jump in! - make as big a splash as you like! See the colour splash up and feel the emotional state take over. See the colour dripping from you as the emotion flows through your body.

Really enjoy it.

If you want to be a little more reserved, just step into the puddle. An alternative is to place the puddle outside a door or on a stage, so that as you walk towards your destination you walk straight through the puddle, seeing the colour splash up as you step into it.

Anchors away!

You remember anchoring? Well, you can set yourself up a number of anchors to trigger particular states. The more you use them, the stronger they become.

You could have one for each different emotional state that will be of use to you, and anchor each one on a different finger, with a different word or with a different colour. You can combine this with the puddle splash described above to have a different coloured puddle for different occasions.

In fact, the puddle splash uses existing colour associations as anchors. You can do the same thing with a favourite piece of music or a word that is associated with the memory or state.

Modelling

Modelling is a very important part of NLP. In fact, purists will tell you that NLP is only modelling, there is nothing else. Everything else that we've talked about is not in itself NLP. NLP is just the process by which we get this expertise out of the heads of experts.

You are an expert. Anything that you can do really well without having to think about it is a talent. Maybe you've had the experience of watching someone do something amazing and asking them "how did you do that?" to which they reply "erm...I just did it. Doesn't everyone do it?"

Many people assume that this means the behavioural knowledge required to perform a complex task is locked away and is irretrievable. We get a glimpse of the knowledge through observing behaviour, but there is no way to extract the knowledge itself. Other people went on to guess at the behavioural programming, based on their observations. They made one key mistake - they tried to guess "why" the individual behaved that way instead of asking "how". "Why" is irrelevant. If I want to copy your talent for writing music, or sticking to a diet, or remember people's names at a party, I don't need to know why you do it. I just need to know how, so I can learn to do it.

Traditional "body language" is an example of this, where a particular movement "means" something specific such as arrogance or fear. Body movement is not a language in itself, it's a component of communication. The effects of "body language" training are still with us today, lingering on in presentation skills courses that teach people how to stand so that they look confident. Isn't it better just to be confident, and let your body language naturally reinforce that?

The originators of NLP, John Grinder and Richard Bandler, decided that all the behavioural psychologists were missing something important. Instead of watching how someone performed a complex task, they just went and asked them. Did they get the "erm..." answer? Well, at first they did but then they developed a way of asking that was new and effective.

Bandler and Grinder were first interested in excellent communicators in the field of personal change, so they went to talk to some of the most outstanding therapists at the time. They found that these people had certain things in common to do with they way that they communicated. By exploring these similarities, a model was developed of the way these people used language to influence patterns of thought and behaviour.

So, all the stuff about anchoring and senses and storytelling is just NLP applied. It's not strictly NLP itself. NLP is the process by which we found out how to do those things by talking to experts.

I'm not going to go into modelling in much detail here, as it could easily fill a book much larger than this one all by itself. There are so many books around on modelling and it's not the subject of this one. So why mention it? Well, because modelling is more of a mindset of curiosity than an explicit set of tools that you must use as prescribed. This mindset will help you to learn interesting things from experts, from other trainers, from delegates and from yourself.

You probably already know about learning styles. What are you? Have you done one of those online tests that tell you how you learn? Well, I suspect you already know how you learn. As Harry Hill said, "you can tell a lot about people from what they're like".

As with all "personality tests", they're not true. They represent a way of thinking about and categorising a certain type of behaviour. If there were four learning types, you would see people everywhere fitting neatly into the four types. If there were eight, you would see....well you get the idea. Personality types are a filter through which you can view the people of the world. They are not true, in and of themselves because there are only two types of people in the world - those who think that there are two types of people in the world and those who don't.

When you watch your delegates, you will notice that they do certain things in a certain order. You will be able to watch the process by which they individually learn. In the appendix, there are some exercises that you can use. Try the one about juggling for a demonstration of learning patterns. Some people will go into a corner, others will form groups. Most of them will stand up and move about. If you watch people with the curiosity of the NLP modelling mindset, you will notice patterns in the way that people learn. These patterns will help you to help people learn. After all, that is your job, isn't it?

Here are a few ways that you can approach modelling. Choose what works best for you.

The logical levels approach

Simply use the Logical Levels hierarchy as a structure for asking questions, so that you guide your interviewee through a sequence of thoughts and experiences. This approach works well for skills that are highly unconscious - the person doesn't know they do it - as you can start at a very abstract level and gradually work down until you get the answers you need to create your model for the skill.

Environment	Where and when do you do it?
Behaviours	What specifically do you do? If you were going to teach me to do it, what would you ask me to do?
Capabilities	What skills do you have that enable you to do this? How did you learn how to do this?
Beliefs	What do you believe about yourself when you do this? What do you believe about the person you're doing this with?
Identity	Do you have a personal mission or vision when you're doing this? What kind of person does this make you? Who are you when you're doing this?
Other questions	How do you know that you're good at this? What happened for you to be good at this? What are you trying to achieve when you do this? Who else do you recommend I talk to about this? What is your state when you do this? Do you set any specific outcomes when you do this? How do you know when you've achieved them?

Success Factor Modelling

Robert Dilts is probably the most well known and prolific NLP modeller, having modelled people like Walt Disney and produced models of generic skills such as leadership and creativity.

Dilts' Success Factor Modelling approach requires that you find a number of people who appear to share a common skill or talent. The whole modelling process is as follows:

Interview the individual
Interview the people they work with or relate to
Watch them in their normal environment to confirm the model
Check the model against their peers to benchmark their performance
Check the model against your own peers to check current research or thinking
Check the model against the individual or company's vision - their stated future direction
Check the model against the individual or company's past - their legacy or habits

From all of these separate models you can then refine a model of the specific skill that can be used by anyone to achieve the same results.

Strategy elicitation and the TOTE model

A strategy is a specific sequence of steps that are necessary to perform a particular task. Simply, you take your subject through the skill, step by step, until you have built up a detailed map of the behaviour. For example, a skill for goal setting might break down into:

Visual construct of desired outcome
Kinaesthetic check for congruence of outcome
Visual recall of current situation
Visual construct of steps required to reach outcome
Kinaesthetic check for desire to take action

In other words, the person imagines what they would like to have, feels good about it, imagines the steps they need to take and, if it feels right, they do it.

The TOTE model adds an extra layer of formality to the basic strategy in that it adds criteria for starting the strategy and criteria for ending it. TOTE stands for Test Operate Test Exit, so to the above example it adds "how do you know when you want something?" and "how do you know when you've got it?"

You may also find that your subject has very specific criteria for the Test and Exit stages, for example someone who is scared of public speaking may know to get scared if there are more than 3 people in the audience. If there are fewer than 3, it doesn't count as a presentation so the "get scared" strategy doesn't run (the Operate part). This can be a very useful change tool - shifting the criteria so that the problem strategy no longer runs.

The curious approach

This one's easy, yet less structured than the other examples. You simply adopt a highly curious state and ask questions like "Wow! That's amazing, how do you so that?" or "Can you teach me how to do that?" Just explore the talent or skill freely and copy what your subject does, asking them to help coach you into the right state.

This approach also incorporates behavioural modelling in which you allow yourself to copy someone else's behaviour without consciously processing it. It's an excellent way to learn physical activities such as dance steps or martial arts moves. You'll be able to copy the moves very successfully very quickly but if someone asks you how to do it, you might say "I don't know, I just do it!"

Motivation

Opinion seems to be divided over whether the carrot or the stick is best for motivation and some people think "both" is right. It's worth us just applying what we know so far to this important subject.

Motivation is a process that translates thought into action, so the first thing to ask is "what exactly do you want people to do?" You can use various language structures that naturally generate motivation which you can read about elsewhere in this book, including logical levels, moving in time and well formed outcomes. When you choose to generate a feeling of motivation you must be certain that what people do as a result is what you intend, therefore it is most important to start with clear goals.

One of the ways in which personalities can differ and thereby be categorised is the natural direction of motivation. Motivation is always a strong, compelling, positive force. In some people it is generated towards goals and desires and in others it is generated away from things to be avoided. Some people like tidiness, others like avoiding mess. Some people like security, others like to avoid insecurity. In both cases, the motivation is positive. It doesn't involve fear or threat, it just heads in a different direction.

This is very important when you structure your language. If your preference is naturally 'towards' then you are likely to say things like "Do this because the end result will be really great". This will be fairly meaningless to all the 'away from' people who like to hear things like "Do this because it will save you work later".

It's very useful to pay attention to what people say when they're listing reasons for decisions or actions. If you tune the direction of your language to theirs, you will simply tell them what they want to hear and reassure them that there is a purpose in what you are asking of them.

When you choose to use either the carrot or the stick, you are choosing between pleasure and pain, desire and fear. By using the stick, you are often threatening to deprive someone of something that they want, or threatening a course of action that they will find unpleasant. "Do this or else..." is a stick command. "If you do this then..." is a carrot command.

As usual, I'm going to leave it to you to decide which, if either, is appropriate for your situation. Neither is right or wrong - it all depends on how you choose which to use. One thing that you should bear in mind is the effect that the carrot and stick have on the brain and in particular the focus of attention. Remember that humans cannot think of doing nothing, they must think of doing something, even if it doesn't seem like much.

When we generalise our own thoughts into language, ambiguous, analogue alternatives tend to take on a binary quality. When you say, "don't drop the glass," you usually mean "hold the glass tight". In a digital, binary system this holds true. In an analogue system like the human brain, the opposite of "don't drop the glass" can be "hold the glass tight", "yesterday" or "a turnip". There are no opposites in an analogue system, only an infinite number of alternatives. An interior designer will tell you that the opposite of red is green, but that's only because they have a frame of reference for colour matching. What is the opposite of a zebra? What is the opposite of Tuesday? With no digital frame of reference, opposites and negatives have no meaning.

The effect of this binary generalisation is that we tend to think of motivation as being linear. We tend to think that people have limited choices because our own choices are limited by what we are currently thinking about.

We tend to think of carrot or stick motivation like this:

In that the person can be motivated to go either one way or the other. This is misleading and leads to expectations that people will do what you want them to when motivated correctly. This is not the case.

Because of the analogue nature of thought, the bizarre way that your focus of attention is pulled from one idea to another from one moment to the next and the fact that, regardless of what you want, other people have needs too, the way that stick motivation works is actually more like this:

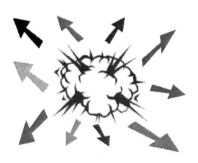

You provide the impetus, the compelling event, the driving force. You light the blue touch paper and retire.

If you're not careful, you will set people off in all directions and they will do some very strange things indeed to avoid what you are threatening them with.

In many companies, I have seen sales people given huge targets and threats of losing their jobs if they don't perform well. Some of them panic and immediately rush off to call customers. Some start ringing recruitment agencies. Some give up all hope and go home. Some go to the pub to drown their sorrows. Some laugh. Some cry. Only a small minority actually do what was intended - work harder.

Conversely, this is the effect of carrot motivation:

The carrot gives people a direction and draws them towards your desired outcome.

You already know about how to set goals, use positive language and direct people's attention, so this really shouldn't come as a surprise.

Which of those two is more useful to you? Don't answer now - decide when you need to make the choice, based on the situation that you are in and the information you have then.

Think back to what you learned about logical levels and apply this to motivation. Very often, you'll hear people tell each other to be more positive, or more professional, or more open. This information is absolutely useless because these words mean totally different things to different people.

Imagine a scenario where a manager tells a group of people to be more professional. Some people will dress smarter, some will tidy their desks, some will charge more for their services, some will go on a training course to become experts, some will go to law school and some will start speaking to customers in a more condescending way. Only a few of them will actually do what was intended.

When you want to change people's behaviour, use language at the behaviour level. Tell them what to do, not what to be.

For the people who are motivated towards outcomes, you need to tell them what will happen if they do what you ask. For the people who are motivated away from problems, you need to tell them what they will avoid if they do what you ask. To make sure you cover everyone, use both:

"By using this method, you'll reach the goal more quickly and avoid some common mistakes"

"When you use what you've just learned about motivation, you'll be able to motivate people more easily and avoid resistance more often, creating a more effective and less stressful learning environment."

Finally, it's worth bearing in mind that if your requests for action are reasonable, and people can see benefits for themselves, people generally don't need much encouragement to take action.

 Remember - there's one easy way to get people to do what you want - TELL THEM WHAT YOU WANT!

I'll go halves with you

Does your brain really have two halves? Here's an image of the brain, looking down from the top:

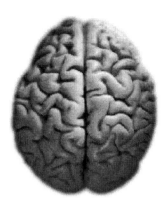

You can see that the two halves are separate - in fact they are connected at the base by a bundle of nerves called the Corpus Collosum.

The question is whether the two halves have identical functions or whether they are specialised into a "creative" side and a "logical" side. The left half of your brain is wired up to the right side of your body and the right half of your brain is wired up to the left side of your body. Brain scans show different areas becoming active for different tasks, but we really can't say for certain that the brain is organised so neatly into creativity and logic. In fact, brain areas can easily reorganise to work around disease or injury, and people who have major strokes or other damage very early on in life recover full functionality so it's possible that the two hemispheres are designed for redundancy rather than differentiation, just like your lungs or kidneys.

Some scientists currently believe that the two halves of our brains are partly specialised to perform different tasks. There are a number of ways that we can demonstrate the way that the brain is organised.

Another model of brain organisation has us equipped with multiple intelligences. Again, these may just be another filter or generalisation. On the other hand, they provide a useful framework for ensuring that learning is presented to take advantage of all of our mental processes. The more ways you learn something, the easier it is to remember.

Sensory systems play a major role in memory and recall. Visual memories are easy and quick to access and allow the learner to view large amounts of information together. Auditory memories are typically accessed at the start and played through like a tape, so it's hard to access information randomly. Try remembering the eighth word in your favourite song without playing it from the start. Kinaesthetic memories take a long time to access and tend not to contain specific information. Kinaesthetic memories are often used by medical students who can be seen moving their joints and prodding themselves during exams. When you go in through your front door at night, does it open in to the left or the right? Ask several people this question and you will see some of them moving their arms as if opening the door - a kinaesthetic memory in action.

If you're interested in multiple intelligences, they are:

Visual/spatial	Good at understanding images, icons, graphics or maps. Good at manipulating images internally and visualising.
Logical/mathematical	Good with numbers, logic problems, deduction, reasoning.
Auditory/musical	Good at remembering tunes, rhythm. Hears tone of voice more than words.
Auditory/language	Good with words, anagrams, crosswords. Able to use indexes easily. Hears content rather than tone of voice.
Interpersonal	Good at interpreting relationships, empathic with others.
Intrapersonal	Aware of internal processes and feelings. In touch with self.
Kinaesthetic	Good with anything physical e.g. learning dance steps or martial arts
Natural	Enjoys the natural world, understands ecology, can name plants.

There were originally seven intelligences in the work of Dr Howard Gardner, the Natural intelligence was added recently.

Many of these overlap onto the basic sensory preferences. For example, people who are good at maths and logic usually have a highly refined visual strategy - they see the numbers or solutions in their heads. This implies that you can take people who are poor spellers or mathematicians and teach them a better strategy. This is actually very easy to do and will bring you good results very quickly.

You have no doubt heard about learning styles and personality types and lots of other categorisation methods. What all of these methods do is generalise human capability into categories. You don't need to worry about labelling people being bad or wrong - it's just a by-product of the way that our brains are wired to use language to code our experience. For example, think about two identical chairs. They are both chairs. Think about two different chairs. They are still both chairs. In fact, the first two are as different as the second two, they're just different in different ways.

We use the word "chair" as a short cut to the sensory experience that we get from the object, but that sensory experience is not the object, just as you can't sit on the word "chair". Labelling and categorising is a natural process, but sometimes it gets out of hand. If we label a chunk of the population as "reflectors" and expect them to learn in only one way, we can expect them to behave how we expect them to. All of these categories are a more accurate description of how you think than about the people you are describing. Categorisation and labelling gives away much more information about your filters on the world than about the people in the world. In fact, there are around 6 billion learning styles and personality types in the world, but thinking about it that way can make it harder to design training courses in the traditional way.

So, however your brain is organised it's a good idea to use all of it. It doesn't matter which organisation model you prefer - what's important is that you have a way of reminding yourself to engage all of the learner's processing power.

 Traditional 'teaching' often hooks into mental processes such as logic and language. Other processes such as music and abstract thought are often linked with creativity. By using both sides of the brain or all intelligences, the learner is able to exploit the specialised capabilities of each, multiplying their learning power.

Of course, it is quite possible to be both logical and creative, if we define creativity as:

"A mental process that gives rise to a new idea"

Or even as:

"The process of finding a solution to a problem that is qualitatively different to a logical progression of the problem itself."

In other words, finding solutions that are different to what you'd find if you just extended the problem logically.

We as human beings have evolved the ability to create solutions to problems which are different to what might be arrived at simply by linear extension of the problem. You have probably seen animals trying to solve a problem such as opening a door by trying the same thing, again and again. Sometimes they are successful through persistence. Human beings can sit back and reflect on the problem and create new solutions that are different, for example go a different way, pull the door instead of pushing. We all have this creative ability, whether we regard ourselves as 'creative' or not. In fact, the word 'creative' has become so closely connected with the arts that many people do not regard themselves as creative just because they can't draw in the way that they would like to.

The important point for you is that, in order to engage all mental processes, both halves of the brain must be engaged.

How? Well, you can use music and rhythm and charts and logic and physical movement. Or, if that's not appropriate in your context then you can make sure that you use lots of colour and pictures. If you're thinking "Ha! But he's not using much colour" then you need to see the cost of colour printing!

You may or may not believe that your brain is specialised into halves, in fact some recent research suggests that most activities take place across the brain rather than being localised. This ties in with some quite old theories of memory which said that the brain works holographically - every memory is stored in every cell and with more connections or more cells comes faster access to those memories. As brain cells die off as we get older, memories don't disappear, they just get harder to access. There may be some truth in this too, but the reality is that no one knows for sure what happens.

Whether you believe in two halves or not, what we can say for certain is that the more of your brain that you use, the better. "Whole brain" exercises can only be good, regardless of how they work, since they exercise your brain differently and get you to make new connections.

So, does the brain have a logical side and a creative side? Personally, I'm not sure but I don't really think it matters. Of what use is that information in the training room, unless you have your electrodes handy to give your delegates' creative halves a zap from time to time?

All of these different theories on brain organisation are very useful to you - not because they're true, but because they encourage you to apply some structure to the way that you create your learning experience to appeal to different learning styles and capabilities. Whichever theory you prefer, you can use it to check that your course design, environment and agenda satisfy the needs of a diverse range of learners. That can only be a good thing!

You may also have heard of "brain gym" or "educational kinesiology" which uses physical exercise to influence brain function. All of these ideas certainly help, and it doesn't take much for you to try a few out and decide for yourself which you like best.

Unless you're training cookery, wine tasting or perfume mixing, the chances are that your audience will be mostly gathering information using three of their many senses:

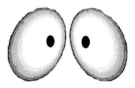 

Although we could also say that language is a special, additional sense.

Any one person will be preferring one of these, the whole audience will be a mixture and any one person will change from time to time. So, how can you structure your delivery to supply the maximum information to your audience, given that you have a natural preference too?

The answer is that you must structure your communication to appeal to all three of these sensory systems. You must also pay attention to times that the audience shifts from one system to another. You will find that you can influence this shift, and use it to communicate more powerfully. Here's how.

Firstly, how do you know which sensory system a person is using? Remember that the brain is gathering information using all of your senses, the preferred sense is the one that you are currently attending to consciously. Don't assume that it's connected to the training material, as we all have the ability to translate sensory information. Right now, you could be seeing the words, hearing them in your head or deciding how you feel about them.

As you might expect, NLP has special words for these three senses. They are Visual, Auditory and Kinaesthetic. In fact, NLP has a special phrase for the word 'sense'. It is 'representational system' and it is meant to indicate that our senses are not reality, they only represent reality.

 Our senses are not reality, they only represent reality. Therefore, they may or may not represent the same version of external events as other people's senses. None of us can claim to have a full version of external events, as there is just too much information to handle consciously.

The internal processing of the brain is available to you externally as a set of 'symptoms'. Here are the ones that we know about today - you may find some new ones:

Language

As you will know, a proper grammatical language structure contains lots of words that don't add anything to the meaning. In other words, meaning not need grammar. It is these non-essential words that we're interested in. How many ways do you hear people say, "I understand"? Do these sound familiar?

I get it
I see
I hear you
That's crystal clear
That's clear as a bell
I can grasp that
That sounds good
I'm with you
I dig
Looks great

When you hear these, you probably translate them all into a confirmation of understanding, rather than paying attention to the particular words used. Well, start paying attention! Here are those phrases again, with their associated sensory system:

I get it	Feel
I see	See
I hear you	Hear
That's crystal clear	See
That's clear as a bell	Hear
I can grasp that	Feel
That sounds good	Hear
I'm with you	Feel
I dig	Feel
Looks great	See

When you next watch the news on TV, or listen to it on the radio, pay special attention to the unscripted interviews. Listen out for people using these words and their language will come alive with a new depth and meaning. Once you have had some practice at this, start matching their language up with the physiological symptoms described below. Of course, you can try this with real people too, it's just that people on TV don't seem to mind as much when you stare at them.

All of this is useful, not in categorising people, but in communicating with them more effectively. You may have heard people labelled as "visual" as if they are only able to understand pictures. In fact, everyone uses all of their senses. Imagine listening to a presentation in a language that you can speak, but not fluently. You translate in your head as much as you can, but after a while you can't help letting your mind wander as you get tired. The same thing happens even when you communicate using the same language, so we are talking about a degree of refinement here which will add to and enhance your existing skills.

Here's a bigger list of words that will help you discover a person's preferred sensory system. Preferred doesn't necessarily mean "always use", think of it as meaning "using right now". I'll use the NLP headings for this list.

Visual	Auditory	Kinaesthetic
See	Listen	Feel
Picture	Hear	Touch
Look	Sound	Grab
Watch	Noise	Hold
Perspective	Loud	Contact
Vision	Quiet	Push
Outlook	Amplify	Embrace
Bright	Tell	Warm
Clear	Resonate	Cold
Focus	Hum	Sinking
Sharp	Whistle	Down
Background	Whine	Ache
Shine	Roar	Gut reaction
Reflect	Silent	Queasy
Dim	Rhythm	Steady
Hazy	Melody	Stable
Short-sighted	Harmony	Solid
Blinkered	Talk	Firm
Colour	Language	Soft
Envisage	Volume	Grasp
Overlook	Wavelength	Handle
Imagine (from Image)	Call	Forceful
Clarify	Say	Smooth

Physiology

To a highly visual thinker, kinaesthetic thinkers appear to be slow and boring. The kinaesthetic thinker might feel that the visual thinker is too flighty, never settling on a particular idea or topic or conversation and talking too fast to pay much attention to.

Visual thinkers see a constant movie in their heads, so their language has to keep up. Strongly visual thinkers hardly ever finish a sentence, as the generation of words just can't keep pace with the images they're trying to describe. They breathe high and fast to keep up with their fast pace of speech, and their hand gestures show you what they are talking about. To make upward eye accessing more comfortable, they look up and lean back a lot, often supporting the backs of their heads with their hands when they are thinking very intensely.

Auditory thinkers hear a constant, harmonious flow of words and sounds. They tend to breathe regularly from the centre of their chest and their gestures add impact and emphasis to their words, much like the conductor of an orchestra. They talk smoothly and freely and you can hear a definite music to their speech, marking out sentences and phrases. Auditory thinkers tend to sit upright and when thinking intensely will often tilt their heads to one side.

Kinaesthetic thinkers base their language on their feelings, so they constantly check their internal feelings and sensations to verify what they are saying. Feelings move much more slowly than words or pictures, so a kinaesthetic thinker will tend to pause a lot and speak without making much eye contact. They tend to breathe slowly and deeply from their stomachs, and their rate of speech is much slower than the other two sensory thinking modes. Their hands will often be still, or they will touch themselves to stay "in touch" with their feelings. Kinaesthetic thinkers tend to lean forwards when thinking as this makes their downward eye accessing more comfortable.

During the course of a conversation, you will move freely between these different modes, although you will tend to prefer one as a "default" mode.

You'll find that, when you're deeply in rapport with someone, your physical posture and breathing will be closely matched. Consequently, you will both be thinking in the same sensory mode. Next time you're in a social environment like a pub, watch out for people who are this deeply in rapport. The first thing you'll notice is the similarity of their posture, but this is not the most important thing to pay attention to. Instead, notice the pace and rhythm of their movements. Notice how they are both using the same type and range of gestures, so that they are either both pointing to the same picture, both conducting the same orchestra or both checking the same kinds of feelings. Essentially, they have entered a shared world - a bubble, within which they seem to have an almost telepathic connection.

Just watching this process in some detail will give you everything you need to know about the role your senses play in creating a shared reality for you and your delegates.

There are a number of elements in physiology, so we'll cover each one separately, looking at the "symptoms" that relate to each sensory system.

	Posture	**Breathing**	**Hand gestures**
See	Leaning back, head tilted up, hands often behind head	High in chest, fast and shallow	Moving quickly, "drawing" the object or events being described. Pointing to specific locations in space related to particular times or emotional states.
Hear	Sitting upright, head tilted to side	Middle of chest, regular and moderate	Moving smoothly, 'conducting' or demonstrating the rhythm of speech or punctuation.
Feel	Sitting forwards, head titled down or down to right	Low in stomach, deep and slow	Relatively still, often in lap or clasped together. Touching body frequently.

Eye movement

Seeing

Hearing

Feeling

Listening to
voice in head

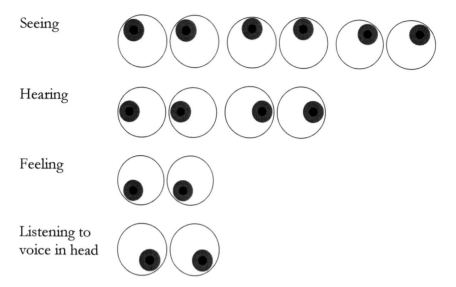

In general, movement to the left infers the recall of an existing memory whilst movement to the right infers the construction of a new experience. Contrary to what the members of some security forces are told, this doesn't apply to everyone, and it certainly doesn't mean that someone is lying, just because they're making new pictures in their head. With some people, the left to right accessing is exactly reversed so, once again, it's important to pay attention to the person in front of you, not the generalisation.

If you want to test this out, find yourself a willing subject and sit down, face to face somewhere quiet. You can ask them these questions, or make up your own more relevant questions. The important thing about this exercise is that they don't have to answer you, they only have to process the question.

You should memorise each question and then look the person right in the eye as you ask it. If you read from the page, you will miss the eye accessing as it will happen as soon as the person understands the question - which is long before you have finished reading it.

- What colour is your bedroom?
- Where is the bed in relation to the window?
- What would your bedroom look like if it were pink? (i.e. not the current colour)
- When you pull back the curtains, what sound do they make?
- What sound would they make if you pulled them back twice as fast?
- What sound would they make if you pulled them back half as fast?
- What do they feel like?
- How easily do the curtains move?
- What can you feel with your toes?
- How do you feel when you hear the sound of chalk on blackboard?
- How does your favourite person's voice make you feel?
- Repeat this to yourself inside your head "Mary had a little lamb"
- Repeat this to yourself inside your head, using the voice of Donald Duck "Mary had a little lamb"
- What's the thing you enjoy doing most?

You will probably notice your subject's eyes moving about rather than going to one place and staying there. This is an example of something known as a 'pattern'. For example, if you asked the question "How easily do the curtains move?", your subject may look up to the left, then up to the right, then down to the right before answering. This indicated them trying to remember seeing their curtains move, then making up a picture of their curtains, then finally checking the image against the feelings in their muscles. You can check your interpretation with them after they answer the question.

As you might suspect, all of these are related to each other. If someone is making pictures in their head, their eyes move up so to get comfortable they lean back. In order to keep pace with the rapidly moving pictures in their head, they have to talk fast and this is supported by rapid, shallow breathing which comes from the upper ribcage. If someone is concentrating on feelings, they look down and to really concentrate hard they lean forwards. Feelings change much more slowly than pictures, so their breathing becomes deep and slow to quieten any movement in their bodies, allowing them to really focus on their feelings.

 You may have already noticed that I seem to say the same thing in a number of ways. This helps to make communication loud, clear and easy to grasp. In other words, it helps you see what I mean, hear what I'm saying and get the hang of it.

Are you getting the picture yet? Does it ring a bell? Do you get it?

This is an easy way for you to communicate with a group of people who are each attending to you with their eyes, their ears and their feelings.

Now that we've been through all that, I can reveal the secret to you:

Don't worry about it. I mean, don't give it any further thought.

What's more important is that you pay attention to your audience's state and that you notice when the state shifts. If you spend all your time trying to work out people's eye accessing, you're missing the point of paying more attention to other people.

My advice on this whole chapter is to simply be aware that people do not speak the same language as you do, even though it sounds the same. Language conveys experience and other people's experiences are not the same as yours. Pay attention to the differences and use them to become a more effective, more empathic communicator.

Whatever you do, don't

Before we start, don't think of a pink elephant, don't notice that itch and whatever you do, don't make a mistake.

Our brains are analogue computers. In practice, this means that, like Roman numerals, we cannot represent zero. We can only represent the absence of something within a framework of the thing that is missing.

Here is an empty box.

What was in it?

Here is another empty box.

What was in it?

So, hopefully you get the idea.

Computers work digitally, so computers can quite happily cope with "not zero", which is most definitely the number one. Analogue computers struggle to understand "not zero" as it essentially means "anything at all except zero" – for example one, two, a hundred, a tomato, a goldfish or an itch. Are you starting to understand the problem with the word don't? Well, don't worry about it too much if you're not.

Have you ever said something like that in a learning context? Don't worry, don't try too hard or maybe even "don't do that."

There are two fundamental problems with the word don't. The first is that our brains cannot make sense of the language without first representing that thing that the word "don't" applies to. In order to decode the language "don't drop the glass" your brain first has to have a representation of what dropping the glass is like in order to know what not dropping it means. That thought alone leads to tiny, involuntary relaxation of the muscles in your hand as you make a picture of the glass dropping. The result? You drop the glass.

The second problem is that telling someone what you don't want them to do gives them absolutely no useful information about what you do want them to do. Ask a decorator to paint your bedroom "not blue" if you want to test this out. At best, you will create confusion. At worst, you'll get a punch on the nose.

Of course, your objective may be to create confusion, in which case don't think about applying any of the information in this chapter.

Whilst our brains are analogue computers, they do operate within rules of context. If you tell someone "don't use a red pen" then they will create a list of alternative behaviours constrained by the context of the language. They will guess that you either mean use a green/blue/black pen or that you mean use a red pencil/crayon. If you say, "don't do that" then they will search for a meaning based on "what am I doing right now?"

If you ask someone to stop an annoying habit by saying, "don't do that" then they will have no context on which to base alternative behaviour. The habit is unconscious – that's what makes it a habit – so they have no awareness of what they are doing.

If you catch yourself saying "don't", quickly backtrack inside your head to figure out how you have decided on this course of action. Usually, you will have made a picture, sound, voice or feeling inside your head of how things may turn out for the worst. Go back to that worry state and pick a more useful, specific outcome. Now follow up your "don't" command with a "do" command.

Here's an example:

1. Watch a group of people working on a lively exercise dangerously close to the projector
2. Make a picture in your head of them knocking it over
3. Say "don't knock the projector over"
4. Realise you said "don't"
5. Backtrack to the picture in your head
6. Choose an alternative, positive outcome
7. Make a picture in your head of that outcome
8. Describe the picture - for example, "move away from the projector"

So you avoid the usual "What projector?" ... Bang ... "Oh, that projector ..." that often happens just after step 3.

Now, once you get the hang of telling people what you want you can start being more creative with your use of the word "don't". For example, if you tell someone "don't forget", you can imagine the result you might get. You could have some fun with this, and it's an interesting way to experiment with motivating people, but don't start thinking about all the ways you'll use what you've learned just yet.

In a nutshell

NLP is about your brain, language and your senses. Everything that is in your brain got there through your senses and is represented by your senses as an incomplete representation of the real world. You brain makes up for its inability to process all of the available sensory data by comparing what is really happening with what it expects to happen and then improvising to hide any differences. In order to make sensory data match with your memory of the world, your brain ignores, corrupts and simplifies sensory data.

If your senses are your brain's input then language is one of your brain's outputs. You were able to communicate very effectively with anyone who took notice of you, long before you learned to speak. The fact that you are alive today proves that you were able to get your own way without the need to learn a spoken language. Strangely, we are brought up to value spoken or written language above other forms of communication, so we are taught to logically exclude or ignore non-verbal language. Our brains, however, have evolved to use non-verbal communication to carry the majority of communication traffic to and from other people. Therefore, we must be aware of this and pay as much attention to non-verbal language as we do to verbal language. Of course, you don't have to actively pay attention to it - you just have to be aware that it's there and that it's feeding your sense of intuition. Learn to trust it.

In other words, spend at least an equal amount of time preparing what you are going to say as how you are going to say it. If you are unprepared, unsure or even doubtful about what you are presenting, your non-verbal communication will reveal your true thoughts to your audience. Some will ignore this, some will dismiss it as intuition and some will attend to it as the primary message - totally ignoring your carefully prepared words.

In order for you to be at your best as a professional communicator, it helps for you to have a variety of ways to manage your own state. You can use a combination of physiology and anchoring to make sure that you maintain your peak state at all times - whatever that may be.

NLP has some really effective and unique communication tools that can help you in any situation, from informing all the way through to influencing. These communication tools tap into natural mental processes and can generate curiosity, motivation and the enthusiasm to go out and take action, right away.

NLP isn't something that you "do" or that you add to your existing skills. It certainly contains some tools and methods which people recognise as being part of NLP, but in itself it doesn't really exist. NLP is just a means to refine what you already do, it isn't something that is separate to your existing skills. Think of NLP as a performance tune up rather than a shiny new toolkit.

Many people who go through the NLP Practitioner training spend some time "doing" NLP to all their friends and colleagues, which can give NLP a bad name. After they've had time to integrate their new skills, most return to their original state with some new enhancements. They're the same person they were before, but they seem to be better at getting what they want from life. NLP is definitely a skillset that can and must integrate with your natural personality, otherwise you will spend so much time thinking about doing it that you'll never get round to doing it.

If you read through this book carefully, you'll find it threaded through with NLP in practice - and to read it means that you too are practicing while learning. If you come to the masterclass or even a Practitioner course, you'll get the opportunity to practice with other people and refine your skills even further.

There are a number of books around that aim to teach NLP skills to trainers, but they seem to be aimed at telling you everything there is to know about NLP and not so much about what to do with it. One of the most popular ones is simply a rehashed introduction to NLP with a few examples of training applications thrown in.

This book is different in that it practices while preaching, and it's written with the aim of helping you become a more effective trainer, using NLP as an enabler. You know that NLP is only one approach and there are many more that are equally valid. Therefore my aim isn't to teach you NLP - if that's what you want, go to a Practitioner course. My aim here has been to help you apply NLP in your work, become more effective and perhaps even choose to learn more about it in the future.

If you're the sort of person who is naturally curious, if you believe you never stop learning and if you have a passion for self improvement, then NLP is one set of tools that can really benefit you.

As you begin to notice more and practice more, you might find yourself dipping back into this handbook for a reminder. As you do, you might notice how the principles and concepts of NLP are woven through it. You can take this as a sign that the principles are also becoming woven through you, helping you to become the teacher, trainer, presenter, coach, facilitator or learning enabler that you have always had the potential to be.

Appendices

Here's some additional information that didn't really fit into the book.

You can use the training exercises freely, although if you publish them yourself e.g. in training notes, I would appreciate a mention. More importantly, I would love to hear how you've used them and what results you have had.

Whilst this isn't strictly a book about NLP in itself, I thought a little background information on NLP and NLP training would be useful.

Finally, there are some useful quotes, a little something about me and some words on the people who have helped this book become reality.

Training Exercises

Here are some ready-made exercises that you can use to demonstrate particular learning points. Some of them are designed to help people learn how to learn, which is a very useful thing to do.

The most important thing to remember about these exercises is that they get the audience *doing* something. It doesn't matter what your training course is about, you must get the audience out of their chairs and moving. Physiology is such a major factor in mental and emotional state, so if you let people sit still for long, their brains will grind to a halt. You may be training computing skills or time management or presentation skills, and you may think that some topics lend themselves well to delegate activity and some don't. As a trainer or teacher, if you're doing more than 50% of the work, you're making life hard for yourself.

You could have people come up with acronyms or mnemonics for existing factual information, or you could create a "learning wall" where people post sticky notes with new ideas that they've had whilst learning. What's important is that the process is creative, and the learners have to physically move to complete it.

Some people can only learn by doing. Simply watching and listening is insufficient.

You can use these exercises as they are described here, or you can adapt them to your own needs. Whatever you do with them, remember to use them, enjoy them, and let me know how you get on!

Open for business

This isn't an exercise as such, but it is a useful hint for getting people focussed at the start of a training course. If you are training within a company you will often find that there are implicit behavioural rules about training courses. For example, break times are flexible, it's OK to leave mobile phones switched on and emails are more important than getting back to the training room on time. If you find these rules distracting, you can bypass them for the duration of the course and set your own rules. To do this, you use a combination of anchoring and pacing in order to gain rapport.

First, pick a spot in the room that you will not stand in again. Now go and stand in that spot. Tell the audience that you want to make sure you understand the way courses have been run before, whilst pointing to the past. This will usually be behind the audience or over to their left, so it's up to you to decide how subtle you can be.

Ask the audience about each rule that you want to 'suspend'. Often, when you raise a rule such as mobile phones or break times, an argument will break out. Let it run its course as rules imposed by the audience have a power of their own.

As you repeat each rule back to the audience, point down to the floor to anchor that rule to your current location.

When you have extracted all the rules you want to suspend, and the audience are firmly embedded in their memories, walk away from the spot and, pointing back at it, say something like "OK, so that's how training courses have been run here in the past". Moving towards the spot where you'll be for the rest of the day, say "So that we can get the maximum value from this shared experience, we're going to do a few things differently. After the course, you can have your old rules back, if you think you still need them." Now, you can list any changes you want to make to the "rules".

A good way to deal with the problem of mobile phones, emails and missing delegates is to say "I know that you are all busy and that you have many demands on your time. I also know that you are here right now because at this moment, this is the most important place for you to be. When we take a break I will tell you the time that I will restart. If you're not back in time I will presume that at that moment, you have something more important that you need to do. I'm happy with that, because I want to make sure that when you're in the room you can be 100% focussed and when you're out of the room it's because you have to do something that is more important for you."

So, you're pacing their current experience and expectations and then leading them in a new direction with suggestions and anchoring. Outside of the training room they can think about work and other 'normal' things, but when they're inside training room it's time to focus and learn.

The majority of delegates will agree that time is valuable and it's important to get the most out of the learning opportunity, and group influence (peer pressure) will do the rest for you.

Learning to learn

Group size: 1

Time: 20 minutes + 10 minute debrief

Materials: Juggling balls, one set per person or A4 paper, three pieces per person

As the Sphinx said in the film Mystery Men, "Before you can learn my teachings, I must first teach you how to learn". I recommend you watch this film as an exercise in running mystical training events.

We all take it for granted that we learn, and we often assume that everyone learns the same way. Most of the training rooms I have ever seen seem to be designed on the basis that we all learn best when we sit at a desk for hours on end, in a darkened room, facing a bright light source where we are shown strange images, accompanied by the hypnotic droning of the air conditioning and the presenter. This may explain why some presenters say, "if you only take one thing away from today then I've done a good job". In an environment like this, transferring just one idea into each delegate's brain is an outstanding feat.

If you have juggling balls, give one set to each person and set them the task of learning how to juggle in 20 minutes.

If you don't have juggling balls, give each person three pieces of paper and have them start by making their own juggling balls. They may hold together better if they put some tape round them.

Finally, stand back and watch. You will notice a number of interesting things happening. Firstly, there will be some negotiation to establish who in the room already has the necessary skills. Some people will go to a quiet corner, others will form groups. Some people will start coaching others, offering advice or feedback. Some will tell others how to do it, others will ask how to do it. Some people will try to tackle the whole task, some will break it down into chunks. Some will start juggling one ball, others will go for all three.

In this simple exercise, you will see patterns emerge for leadership, coaching and learning styles. What's more important is that everyone gets up and moves about in order to learn. Movement is a key part of learning.

Another key learning point is to notice what happens when people drop the juggling balls. Do they stop? Do they give up in despair? Do they even notice or draw attention to it? Does this mean that making mistakes is just a sign that learning is taking place?

Please don't run this exercise and then have the audience sit down at a desk for the rest of the day. Use what you have learned and incorporate it into the whole experience.

Learning under pressure

Group size: 1

Time: 20 minutes + 10 minute debrief

Materials: A4 paper, one piece per person

Some people say they learn best when under pressure or against deadlines. Certainly, we can learn important lessons at a time of heightened stress but we rarely learn complex tasks or retain information effectively.

Give each person a piece of paper and have them make a paper aeroplane. At the end of the 20 minutes, there will be a competition. The winner gets a prize and the loser pays a penalty. If you wish, and if you have enough paper, you can allow people to test as many designs as they like but they may enter only one for the competition.

Again, just stand back and watch.

At the end of the time, hold the competition and award points for each aeroplane.

If you are feeling brave, you can add an extra layer to the exercise at this stage. For some people, you decide the points and make them arbitrarily high or low. For other people, let the audience choose the points awarded. You may choose to give away real prizes but I recommend that you give the winner the prize of one minute imagining the holiday of their dreams and the loser the penalty of one minute imagining the booby prize of their dreams.

You will have noticed some interesting things happening in this exercise that didn't happen during the juggling exercise. Firstly, the threat of competition reduces the amount of collaboration. Secondly, the threat of a prize or penalty will focus attention in one direction or the other. Ask each delegate whether they were motivated to win the prize or avoid the penalty.

How does the concept of "winning" affect the way that people deal with "failure", compared to in the juggling exercise?

During the judging stage, you will see different patterns of behaviour too, depending on whether you or the audience awarded the points. People seem to take ownership and responsibility for decisions they have been involved in, and you will learn about the influence hierarchies of the group.

You can ask people during the debrief whether they were thinking about the prize or the penalty and the answers will reveal interesting information about the way that people are motivated - some towards desires and some away from threats.

Of course, you'll notice lots of other things too. Again, it's important that you incorporate what you notice into the whole experience. Some people think that prizes and competitions are motivating. Now that you have tried both ways, you can decide for yourself before having a "fun quiz" at the end of the training course.

You'll notice that it doesn't matter who "wins".

Negotiation

Group size: 2

Time: 10 minutes + 10 minute debrief

Materials: Record cards, sticky notes or a few pieces of A4
                   paper which you'll tear into small pieces

In pairs, delegates will conduct a simple negotiation, e.g. what TV channel to watch, where to go for a holiday or what to have for dinner. The key to this exercise is to have the delegates adopt beliefs and behaviours which are not their own, as they limit their own negotiating ability to ruling out certain approaches and behaviours which are quite acceptable for other people.

Create a number of characters and write them onto the cards, giving a card to each delegate so that their partner does not see what is on the card. This is to stop them deciding what is the "right answer" for this exercise. Suggested characters include:

A teenager
A five year old child
A newborn baby
A pensioner
A politician
Someone you know who is very manipulative
Someone you know who always seems to get their own way
Someone you know who uses emotional blackmail
The most inspiring leader you know
The most diplomatic person you know
The most influential person you know

You should probably avoid giving named people as characters as you will limit behavioural choices to the delegate's perception of that person, rather than to your perception of that character, so you will get a result but it won't be the one you intended.

The purpose of this exercise isn't to "win" but to have delegates try on behaviours that they would never normally use or have access to.

During the debrief, you can ask delegates what tactics they normally employ to get compliance from someone, and the answers will include "ask nicely", "bargain", "trade a favour" etc. Then ask them what a five year old child would do and the answers will include "cry", "smile", "sulk" etc. Now, do you know any adults who do any of those things? Of course you do! So, these behaviours can't be ruled out because they work, in the right context. Ruling out choices just limits your ability to achieve your goals.

Whether this implies that the ends justify the means may be an interesting, if lengthy, discussion topic. By this time, they have already used tactics that they "would never use", so it's really too late!

Mediation

Group size: 3

Time: 30 minutes + 10 minute debrief

Materials: Record cards, sticky notes or a few pieces of A4
                   paper which you'll tear into small pieces

This exercise is exactly the same as the previous one except the negotiation group now comprises three people - two negotiating parties and a mediator. The job of the mediator is to find a level at which both parties are satisfied. Compromise is not permitted, both parties must have their original or better criteria satisfied.

Rotate so that each person has a turn as mediator, taking 10 minutes per turn.

This exercise gets people thinking about values. If you wish, you can introduce people to the idea of logical levels first, but they already know it - intuitively. This is a good coaching exercise because it trains people to avoid compromise. In a compromise, neither party is satisfied because each has to settle for less than they want in order to reach an agreement. Did anyone in the audience notice that, with a mediator in place, there was no longer a requirement on them to reach an agreement so they could be as demanding as they liked?

A coaching approach to this exercise would be for the mediator to ask each person "what's important about what you want, what will it give you, what will it do for you" until a common value is reached. Then, the mediator would move back down, finding examples of activities that satisfied the common value for both parties. For example, the negotiation may be about which TV channel to watch but the outcome may be to go to the cinema instead.

Of course, that's just a good coaching approach. There will be many other approaches which are equally effective. Your job is to draw them out, model them, notice and draw attention to the important lessons and incorporate them into the whole experience.

That's right

Group size: 2 to 20ish

Time: 1 minute per person + 10 minute debrief

Materials: None

Each delegate takes it in turn to stand up in front of the group and speak on any subject at all. The remaining members of the group try as hard as they can to constantly interrupt the speaker with irrelevant questions and comments. The speaker's job is to acknowledge each interruption and move on. The speaker must not engage in a conversation with any interrupter. The speaker's must acknowledge the values of the interrupter but not the interruption. This exercise trains delegates to separate people from their behaviour.

During the debrief, it's interesting to discuss some of the strategies people use to keep themselves on track. I find that the people who are most successful in this exercise are those who use an incongruence technique - they use polite, warm and thankful language and voice tone whilst saying "shut up" with their gestures and body posture.

What do you notice?

Group size: Larger than 3

Time: 30 seconds + 10 minute debrief

Materials: Pen and paper

One person volunteers to give a short presentation lasting only 30 seconds on any subject. Each audience member writes down the first 5 things that they notice.

When debriefing, ask what kind of things people noticed and you'll find that some people notice what they can see - clothing, hand movements, movement etc. Some people notice what they can hear - voice tone, pauses, coughs, accent etc. Very few people will comment on the subject matter unless it is something remarkable or contentious such as football!

If you keep a record of what people notice, you'll see an interesting pattern emerge. Just over half of the items will be visual, about a third will be auditory and the remainder will be specific to the content. I personally think that's a strong correlation with Mehrabian and Argyle's findings on communication channels, so it seems we don't just transmit on those channels, we receive on them too.

If you're interested, their findings were:

Visual 55%
Auditory non-verbal (voice pitch, tone, volume, inflection) 38%
Auditory verbal (words) 7%

This is a great exercise to remind people that getting their state and confidence right is far more important than spending hours writing their presentation slides!

Cheat

Group size: 3 to 6 per pack of cards

Time: 30 minutes + 10 minute debrief

Materials: Packs of ordinary playing cards

In this exercise, groups play the card game called Cheat. This has very simple rules - the pack is shuffled and dealt equally between players and the winner is the player who gets rid of his cards first. Each player, takes it in turn to lay down cards in groups of the same value, such as "three Kings" or "two sevens". The next player can only lay down cards that have the same value or plus or minus one, so if the first player lays down "two sevens" the next player can only lay down sixes, sevens or eights. The cards are placed on a pile in the middle of the table, face down. What happens if a player does not have any cards of the right value? I refer you to the name of the game.

A player can cheat at any time and usually this is detected by the other players counting cards, guessing and reading sensory cues such as giggling or fidgeting. In this exercise, the players must use only sensory cues to determine cheating.

Any player can call "Cheat!" at any time and the person who last laid down cards must show the cards they laid on the pile. If the call of Cheat is correct i.e. the cards are not what they were said to be, the Cheater picks up the entire pile. If the call of Cheat is incorrect i.e. the cards are as called, the caller picks up the entire pile. Play then resumes.

Since the players are relying on sensory information, they are forced to calibrate their senses and will come up with interesting strategies for detecting cheating. The more sneaky players will also develop strategies to avoid detection and even strategies to deceive the other players. During the debrief, it is interesting to compare these strategies to the ways that the players move through their working lives.

Cheat is a game that rarely has a winner because the person with the most cards is always the best placed to identify Cheaters, so only the most skilful players will be able to cheat consistently enough to lose all their cards.

The group sizes are not important, but if you have only two players then each will always know when the other is cheating. If you have too large a group, each player will not have enough cards and will almost always have to cheat. A group size of 4 is ideal, unless you combine multiple packs. The ability to place down "nine Aces" adds an interesting dimension to the game!

Rapport and eye contact

Group size: 2

Time: 10 minutes + 10 minute debrief

Materials: None

In pairs, person A sits comfortably and talks about a subject of interest to them. Person B matches their body posture as much as they can within physical constraints. It doesn't matter whether they copy exactly or adopt a mirror image posture. Person B gives plenty of non-verbal feedback, just like in a real conversation with a friend - nodding their head, smiling etc. When person A is in "full flow", person B changes posture and breaks eye contact.

A and B then swap roles and repeat. At the end, get everyone to make eye contact and smile warmly.

As a facilitator, the hardest part for you is getting people to break eye contact - their eyes will be irresistibly drawn together.

During the debrief, pay attention to the feelings of discomfort experienced by both person A and person B at the point that eye contact was broken. It seems that eye contact is hard wired into our communication ability.

Practice at breaking eye contact is very useful, especially as a means of controlling the flow of a conversation or quietening a noisy delegate!

Rapport and voice tone

Group size: 2

Time: 10 minutes + 10 minute debrief

Materials: None

In pairs, person A says a very short phrase, no more than a couple of words, and person B repeats it back, matching pace, rhythm, tone, pitch, volume and inflection. Person A listens carefully and coaches person B to match the voice tone more accurately. They continue until person B gets it exactly right or close enough, then swap.

A and B then swap roles and repeat. Continue for a few turns and then debrief.

During the debrief, pay attention to any feelings the delegates experienced at the point that person B got the phrase exactly right.

Instant amazement

Group size: 1

Time: 2 minutes

Materials: None

If you want a really quick exercise to make your delegates say "wow!" then here's one that handily demonstrates how your beliefs dictate your capabilities. In other words, you will achieve what you think you will achieve.

All delegates stand up with enough floor space around them to swing their arms freely. You ask the delegates to point directly out in front of themselves, then turn as far as they can whilst keeping their feet still. When they have stretched round as far as they can go, they look down their arms and make a note of something they're pointing at. When they've done that, they turn back to the front and return their arms to their sides.

Next, they can close their eyes if that helps them imagine that they are raising their arms and turning again. This time, they're just going to imagine turning and turning so easily that they feel like they're made of rubber. They go past the point they stopped at before, way past it - maybe two or three or four feet. Now they notice what they're pointing at and when they've done that and returned their imaginary arms to their sides, they can open their eyes again.

Finally, they do the exercise one more time for real, to see how much further round they can turn.

Here are a few more stories for you to enjoy learning from.

Go team

Once, there was a successful businessman who had a hobby that he was very passionate about. In his spare time, he loved motor racing. At first, he used to go along to as many races as he could and watch but as he became more successful, he could afford to take part. He was a very talented driver and quickly built himself a reputation as a serious competitor.

One day, he decided he would take the plunge and dedicate himself to his dream - to build his own racing team. He set aside some money of his own, gained commitment from sponsors and started to recruit his team.

At first, the recruitment didn't go very well. He couldn't afford to pay the same salaries as the top teams paid, so he was looking for talented but unknown drivers. He recruited some, but they didn't stay in the team long before they moved on. Like any manager, he knew that he needed to have a team that worked well together.

The other problem that he had was that he was himself a very accomplished driver. When he recruited a new driver he would try to teach them to drive better. Unfortunately, he didn't really know how he could drive so well as it was mostly intuitive. He would get angry with the drivers when they couldn't see for themselves how he was able to drive. He was on the brink of closing the team down, believing that the problem was one of recruitment.

He was watching a sports program on TV one day when he noticed something odd. When the interviewer was talking to a football manager, the manager kept referring to someone called a 'coach'. The same thing happened with some other sports too. He wondered what a coach could do that a manager couldn't. By chance, he then met someone who was a team coach, so he invited him down to the race track to see what would happen.

The coach watched the drivers practice, and he watched the team manager trying to tell the drivers how to drive. The drivers lacked confidence in their own talents and when they asked how the manager knew certain things, he said "it just feels right", or "you can tell by the way it sounds".

There were three drivers in the team, so the coach watched each one very carefully, and he also watched the manager very carefully. The first driver, Adam, was very good at accelerating. From the starting line, Adam was at least a car's length in front of anyone else at the first corner. He seemed to have an intuitive sense of when to change gear to maximise the car's performance. The second driver, Brian, could brake later than anyone else and so was much faster into the corners than any of the other drivers. He seemed to have an intuitive sense of knowing when to brake as he approached a bend. The third driver, Claire, could take corners faster than any of the other drivers on the circuit. She seemed to have an intuitive sense of the car's cornering ability and grip.

The downside of these talents was that Adam was always the first into the first corner, but the last out. Brian caught up with Adam at the bend but slowed down too much and was overtaken. Claire would overtake on the bend but lose her advantage on the straight.

The coach got the whole team together and pointed out to them their strengths. The drivers began to feel much better about this. Each driver, at a certain point on the track, was by far the fastest driver on the circuit but was let down by average performance in other areas. The coach began to ask some very special questions about how the drivers knew what they knew.

It turned out that Adam was listening for a certain tone from the engine, tyres and gearbox. He could hear when the car was at peak power output and he could change gear at the exact moment to take advantage. Consequently, he accelerated much faster than drivers who only changed gear at the 'red line' by watching the rev counter. With some help from the coach, he was able to teach the other drivers what to listen for.

Brian could brake much later because he was looking somewhere different to the other drivers. The other drivers were looking at the apex of the bend, whereas Brian was looking beyond the bend. He was able to judge the distance to the apex much more accurately, enabling him to brake late but still drive safely. With some help from the coach, he could easily teach the other drivers where to look.

Claire could actually feel the car's sideways motion. She could very accurately feel the movement of the suspension as the car leaned into the bend and she could feel how the motion changed as the tyres started to lose grip. She could actually feel the acceleration at different points in her body. With some help from the coach, she was able to teach the other drivers how to feel the movement of the car.

The team went from strength to strength, not because they were taught something new, but because they were able to share their talents and exploit them for the benefit of the whole team. Each driver still had their unique talent, they just helped each other achieve above average results across the range of skills needed to be successful. The coach didn't need to be an expert in driving, only an expert in learning.

What about the manager? Well, the coach had a special job for him. He had to go to every newspaper, sports journalist, sponsor, TV station and racing promoter and tell them that he had a new team. He had to tell them that this was the best team on the planet and they were going to re-write the motor racing rules. He had to prove to everyone that he believed in them. And so, the new team was reborn.

Working holidays

There was once a salesman for a company that made special metal alloys for weapons. He had travelled the world, selling his company's products to every developed nation. He loved his job and he couldn't help doing it, even on holiday. One year, he took his holiday in the Amazon Rainforest (it could happen!) and he came across a tribe of Indians who were hunters. He asked them what they used for their arrow tips and they said "We hunt a wild cat that lives in the forest. We use its fur for clothing, its meat for food and it's teeth for arrow tips. They are very sharp and easily penetrate the skin of small animals." The salesman asked how many teeth could be used from each cat and they said "Four". Then he asked how accurate their hunters' archery skills were. They said "Every child serves a ten year apprenticeship to become a master archer. If they cannot shoot arrows straight, they run out of cat's teeth and the village people have no meat".

So the salesman immediately recognised a great opportunity, and he also realised that he needed to keep his best product until last so that he could build up his sale. He asked the leader of the village "If I could show you a way to hunt more cats, and bigger animals, with a limitless supply of arrow tips and reduce your apprenticeship for archers to just one year, would you be interested?" The wise, yet strangely gullible village leader said "Of course, can you do a presentation to my board tomorrow?"

So, the salesman showed the villagers arrow tips made from steel. They were heavier than cat's teeth but harder and sharper. They could buy a limitless supply of arrow tips (because they happened to have a gold mine in their village that they didn't understand the value of) so the hunters didn't have to be so accurate. With just some basic training in how to use a bow and arrow, anyone could hunt a cat. The villagers rejoiced.

After a few days, the salesman returned and showed the villagers his titanium alloy arrow tips. They were as sharp as steel yet as light as a cat's tooth. Now that everyone in the village was a hunter, he had more users to demonstrate the product to. Sure enough, the arrow flew further than the steel tipped arrow. To the salesman's surprise, the villagers said "yeah, very nice, but we're happy with our steel arrows". The salesman said "But you'll use fewer arrows because these will fly further" and the villagers said "So?"

The next day the salesman returned with tungsten carbide tipped arrows, and had the same reaction as the day before. He was very confused – normally his customers would be getting more and more excited. He decided to go back to the village and show them his best product. "Look", he said, "I have here arrow tips made with tungsten carbide tips, titanium alloy bodies and with a depleted Uranium filling." He fired one at a tree and it went straight through, like a hot knife through butter. The villagers said "Impressive, but we don't eat trees". Now the salesman was really upset. Couldn't these people see the applications of his marvellous arrow tips? Perhaps they were too stupid too understand. His wife had warned him about this when he left her by the poolside in Rio a week earlier.

The wise village leader said "We can see your arrow tips are indeed marvellous, but remember we are a simple people with simple needs. Your steel arrow tips already represent a step change in technology for us, enabling greater exploitation of our natural habitat without disturbing our learning based culture." It turned out that a management consultant had been on holiday there just the week before. "Your top of the range arrow tips are too advanced for us. We have neither the skills nor needs to exploit their full potential, therefore we only require something that is one level better than what we have today. Besides, I'm going on a dream quest this afternoon and I'll be off my head on psycho-active mushrooms for a few days, so I can't make a decision until next week"

The salesman learned a very important lesson on that holiday - that he shouldn't leave his wife alone in Rio with only a book for company, but that's another story. Do you know what else he learned?

What is NLP?

What is NLP? It's a mindset, an attitude that has created a wide range of techniques that are used in business, coaching, personal change and therapy to solve problems, create changes and help people like you to tap into the vast unconscious resources that lie within you.

In training, NLP is not something that you learn about – it's something that you experience for yourself so that you can learn what works best for you. Some of the exercises will have a huge impact on you, whilst others will seem to have no effect at all. There is no right way to try the exercises, and there is no right answer. What is more important than anything else is that you pay close attention to what happens – whatever happens – and that you are able to learn something from that experience.

NLP is concerned only with what works. The only way you will find out what works for you is to do something and then notice what happens. Just getting into this simple habit will put you way ahead of most of the population. Many people will say "I don't think that would work" instead of trying it. Many more people go through life not noticing what works for them and what doesn't. By practicing these skills so that they become habits, you will get better results than most other people.

NLP isn't something that you learn how to do, it's more a process of refining what you already do so that you get better, more consistent results. By enjoying the learning process, you will find yourself achieving more ambitious goals easily and getting more from life.

NLP is a toolkit for modelling outstanding performance that has been used to create practical toolkits that help you get better, more consistent results in your career and personal life. You can use it to develop your communication skills, relationships, achieve goals and solve many different types of personal and professional problems.

NLP is relevant to you because it allows you to access the skills and resources you already have in a way that makes it easier for you to get consistent results. NLP is not about you learning a whole different way of operating – if anything, it's a way for you to concentrate more easily on what already works for you. Of course, NLP does contain a lot of tools and techniques that you can pick up and use, I'm just guessing that you already use many of them without knowing it.

NLP is not new – it's not a complicated system dreamt up by someone in a dark cave somewhere, it's simply a method of modelling and replicating unconscious, behavioural skills. Over the past 30 years or so, excellent performers in many areas have been modelled to produce techniques. Therapists were originally modelled for their ability to help other people change. Since then, athletes have been modelled for their ability to motivate themselves and reach peak performance states. Sales people have been modelled for their ability to build great relationships and influence the outcome of negotiations. Actors have been modelled for their ability to access states – I heard that Mike Myers uses it to access the different characters he plays in the Austin Powers films. I spend a lot of time working with teams in companies, modelling the high performers and transferring that model to everyone else in the team, so that everyone can get the same results.

You might be wondering what "NLP" stands for – Neuro Linguistic Programming, which simply means that it's the study of the relationship between your brain, your language and your behaviour. It also implies that any unconscious behaviour – something that you can do without having to think about it – is a series of simple programs that can be run without conscious intervention. Driving a car is a good example of a series of programs – changing gear, knowing where to steer etc. – that you mostly control consciously. If you have ever 'missed' part of a journey or had a conversation with someone whilst driving, you'll have an experience of unconscious behaviour.

In the 1960s, Richard Bandler, a mathematician, and John Grinder, a linguist wanted to find out if there was a way of modelling and coding the healing language used by certain exceptional therapists like Milton H Erickson and Virginia Satir who seemed to have a magical effect on people who came to them for help - 'healing' them with just a few words compared to years of repetitive 'traditional' therapy.

Bandler and Grinder did indeed produce such a model and they uncovered some aspects of our use of language which are powerful and surprising. You can read about the original modelling in books such as "Structure of Magic".

They noticed that people such as Erickson and Satir naturally used language to change beliefs and behaviour. Satir asked questions which changed the way people thought. She challenged people's internal beliefs and brought them to the surface where they could be dealt with. When a wife would say, "my husband always comes home late - he doesn't love me", Virginia Satir would ask "how do you know that coming home late means not loving you?". This sounds so simple, yet it's very different from other approaches because it's directed at the world inside someone's mind rather than the "facts" of the matter. Other therapists might have worked on the husband's timekeeping or given the wife a hobby or social life. Virginia made people think differently about their values and beliefs. The wife could feel loved, whatever time her husband came home. That alone changed the balance of their relationship and gave them new choices.

One of Erickson's natural patterns was the use of presuppositions - beliefs we hold true in order for something else to make sense. For example if I say, "how is John?" then I presuppose that John exists and that you know who and how he is. My wife recently had to take a standard test for post-natal depression which had been based on interviews with women who knew how it felt to be depressed. The questions presupposed depression and the only possible outcome was - how much? Many of the questions actually made no sense to her because they related to thoughts and emotions she'd never felt. The test questions all made a presupposition - that the test subject is depressed, even if they don't think so.

As with all NLP, we do this all time - naturally and with random results. You might say to a colleague "you look nice today" and your colleague might think, "Did I look dreadful yesterday?" Someone may say to you "have you seen our new boss yet?" and you think, "We have another new boss?"

I heard a great story about children not going to the dentist early enough because their parents are scared to go. One mother overcame her fear to take her little girl who was naturally curious and open minded - with no preconceived ideas as to what would happen. As she sat in the chair, her mother said "don't worry, it's not going to hurt". How do you think that little girl coped with that experience, given this new piece of information she'd never considered before?

If I say "it should be warm in here by now" then I presuppose that it's cold. If I say "How will you feel when you realise you no longer have that bad habit" then in order to tell me how you'll feel, you must accept that it's possible to change.

When people have problems, they often operate within a restricted model of the world, in that they don't seem to have access to resources and choices that would normally be available. Therefore, there's no point trying to help someone with a problem when you're working from your view of the world - you must work within theirs. This leads to a key principle of NLP - that people with problems are actually working perfectly and making the best choices they can, given their current understanding of their situation. This simple change in perspective leads to outstanding results when NLP is applied in therapy or coaching.

NLP stands for **Neuro Linguistic Programming**. That's quite a complicated term for something that's really quite simple - **Neuro** as in the function of the brain, **Linguistic** as in language and **Programming** as in the following of defined patterns and routines. Think about an activity you perform regularly without thinking about it, for example:

- shaking hands
- drinking a cup of coffee
- saying that little catchphrase you have
- driving a car

All of these activities are incredibly complex in terms of eye and muscle co-ordination, timing etc. Think of all the muscles you use just smiling at someone. You don't need to think about moving all those muscles - you just decide to smile and it happens because somewhere in our brain there is a program, like a computer program, which contains all the commands to build a smile. That's where the **programming** part of NLP fits in. These automatic programs could be called "talents" because they achieve consistent results, yet the person with the talent is often unaware of it.

Talents that produce undesirable results are often called "phobias" and these too can be changed, quickly and effectively, using the NLP toolkit.

So, NLP is a mindset of curiosity and a set of tools and processes designed to bring about rapid and long lasting personal change. Some of these tools have found their way into other disciplines such as education, sales and public speaking.

What all of these areas have in common is the potential to benefit from the sharing of excellence.

You can become a licensed Practitioner of NLP through many training companies now established in the UK and worldwide.

Personally, I work with PPI Business NLP because they have a business background, whereas many of the other training companies in the UK have a therapeutic background and this is reflected in the way that they position and deliver their NLP training. PPI also work with small, interactive groups, which is a great environment to learn NLP in. Some companies run their courses in theatres with hundreds of people. Not surprisingly, these companies favour the "you don't need to ask any questions because you're learning unconsciously" approach. You just need to choose which suits you.

Many NLP training companies are introducing new levels of NLP training, including diplomas, certificates, Business Practitioners and even MSc courses. The fact is that there are only three levels as far as licensing is concerned - Practitioner, Master Practitioner and Trainer. Diplomas and certificates are usually at a foundation level and do not result in licensed certification. The MSc courses typically comprise some HR or management modules wrapped around a Practitioner course. Decide what you want to do with it before you sign up.

The three levels of licensed training are quite distinct in terms of the aims of the training. At Practitioner level, the key aim is to give you a personal experience of change. Before you start learning how to change other people, it's very important that you have a personal reference for the way that people change and how the tools work. You will learn some basic change tools and by the end of the course you will have experienced some kind of personal change such as solving a problem or curing a phobia. At Master Practitioner level, you gain more insight into the structure and application of the tools so that you can create new tools yourself and refine the use of techniques such as hypnosis. At Trainer level, you will learn how to learn about NLP so that you can train others.

You don't need any training at all to use NLP, but you'll only get a license to practice if you complete the course. You need to decide for yourself if that's important to you but I would say that the experience of Practitioner training is far more useful to you than the certificate will be, and it is totally different to just reading a book - even a good book like this!

Practitioner training is a very personal experience - even a journey - and therefore your relationship with the trainers and other delegates is the most important factor. You need to be working with people who you feel comfortable with to get the most out of the training.

Before signing up with any NLP training provider, first go to a free taster session or ask to attend a course for an hour before you make up your mind. Make sure you feel comfortable with the kind of people who attend that course, as this gives you a lot of information about where that trainer positions themselves in the market.

The next question to consider is which certificate to go for. Basically, the Society of NLP was set up by Dr Richard Bandler, co-creator of NLP. Early in 2004, the Association of NLP released a statement recognising Bandler and Grinder as the creators of NLP and therefore the best people to license Practitioners. You also have the PGNLP, INLPTA and some European 'bodies'. The bottom line is this: don't choose NLP training for the certificate – choose it for the most appropriate learning experience for you.

The big fallout between the ANLP people and the SNLP was mainly over course durations. SNLP courses tend to be around 8 days, others around 20 days. The ANLP people say you can't learn NLP in 8 days, the SNLP people say the ANLP people are wasting 12 days of your time. The truth is that it takes a lifetime to learn and integrate NLP, so the course is the beginning of the learning process, not the end of it. 8 days or 20 days make no difference to this, only to the training style.

Finally and most importantly, the training courses are neither the beginning nor the end. The beginning must be an immense curiosity about people and about self improvement. There is no end, because you can always learn something new from everyone you meet.

Useful quotes

Famous people said....why NLP is useful. If you ever suspected that NLP is just advanced common sense, then these wise words may help....

If there is any one secret of success, it lies in the ability to get the other person's point of view and see things from that person's angle as well as your own.

Henry Ford

The greatest discovery of our age has been that we, by changing the inner aspects of our thinking, can change the outer aspects of our lives

William James

Believe you can't, believe you can. Either way you're right!

Henry Ford

Our life is what our thoughts make it.

Marcus Aurelius

When you put a limit on what you will do, you put a limit on what you can do.

Charles Schwab

Obstacles are things a person sees when he takes his eyes off his goal.

E. Joseph Crossman

Chance favours the prepared mind.

Louis Pasteur

As long as you're going to think anyway, think big.

Donald Trump

When you get to the edge, step off...you'll always land somewhere

If you know which musician sang this, let me know!

Trying is the first step towards failure.

Homer Simpson

It is common sense to take a method and try it. If it fails admit it frankly and try another. But above all, try something.

Franklin D. Roosevelt

Nurture your mind with great thoughts, for you will never go higher than you think.

Benjamin Disraeli

Remember, happiness doesn't depend upon who you are or what you have; it depends solely upon what you think.

Dale Carnegie

And my personal favourite....

We are the music makers, and we are the dreamers of dreams.

Willy Wonka

Websites for further reading

Communications In Action is a leading business coaching consultancy. We help you to change the things you didn't know you could change, to get the results you never thought you could get.

www.ciauk.com

Ascent is a unique adventure coaching experience that helps you to explore and realise your dreams.

www.ascent-experience.com

excellerate is a consultancy that helps you apply the principles and techniques of sport psychology in business

www.excellerate.org

The Skills Network is a learning community that supports personal and career development.

www.theskillsnetwork.com

NLP In Business is a knowledge base of research and information on the applications and business benefits of NLP.

www.nlpinbusiness.com

Change Magic is a toolkit for change engineering and organisational problem solving. Visit the site and try out the unique Unsticker - your problem will never be the same again!

www.changemagic.com

Executive and Business Coaching Network is a network of executive coaches.

www.execcoach.net

The PPI NLP Store has a large selection of NLP books and CDs.

www.ppi-nlp-store.com

The Author

Peter Freeth is an internationally acclaimed communicator, coach and explorer of human behaviour. His books have been translated into all known languages and forms of communication, and are a constant companion to many heads of state and celebrities.

Remember, think big!!

Peter Freeth is a leading business coach, trainer, presenter, author and consultant who has a rare mix of communication, technical and business skills and an interest in learning and developing new tools and techniques that help others get the results they want, more easily and more often.

www.ciauk.com

questions@ciauk.com

0870 1620802

+44 870 1620802

Thanks and Dedications

This book is dedicated to Millie, the best trainer in the world because she can teach her parents to do anything, any time without having to use words at all.

I first learned about NLP from a sales trainer at Mercury Communications - John Davies. Over the years, many people including Graham Dexter, Jonathan Altfeld and Michael Beale encouraged me to develop my skills further.

Everyone who supported the NLP in BT Group played a part too, as did all of the wonderful people who presented workshops for us. The NLP in BT Group has now become The Skills Network and continues to live on as personal and professional development community.

The NLP - Skills for Learning masterclass was originally created for people like Lesley Boughton. It developed with the help of Vince Kirkbride and in particular Jan Watts who kept chasing me to run the course! This handbook evolved alongside that masterclass, and grew from seeds planted in other books I'd started work on.

This book grows and changes whenever I find out something new about the way that people learn (or when I find a mistake). I'd love to hear from you if you have something to contribute, and I'd especially love to hear from you if you use something from this book and get great results that you would like to share.

Many people have helped me on my journey – their names would fill another book. Anyone who has ever been on a training course of mine has taught me a lot, and I continue to learn everything I know from the people who think they are learning from me.

Finally, thank you for taking the time to get this far. Without you, I would be talking to myself!